SENSATIONAL
SALADS

SENSATIONAL
SALADS

MORE THAN 75 CREATIVE & VIBRANT RECIPES

KATHY KORDALIS

PHOTOGRAPHY BY
MOWIE KAY

RYLAND PETERS & SMALL
LONDON • NEW YORK

Senior Designer Megan Smith
Senior Editor Abi Waters
Editorial Director Julia Charles
Head of Production Patricia Harrington
Creative Director Leslie Harrington
Food Stylist Kathy Kordalis
Food Stylist Assistant Sadie Albuquerque
Prop Stylist Lauren Miller
Indexer Vanessa Bird

First published in 2024 by
Ryland Peters & Small
20–21 Jockey's Fields, London
WC1R 4BW
and
341 E 116th St, New York
NY 10029
www.rylandpeters.com

10 9 8 7 6 5 4 3 2 1

Alongside the new recipes in this
book are those previously published in
*Party Food to Share, Roast Revolution,
Cauliflower Power, Rice & Grains* and
Mediterranean Summer Table.

Text © Kathy Kordalis 2024
Design and photography
© Ryland Peters & Small 2024

ISBN: 978-1-78879-594-4

Printed in China

A CIP record for this book is available
from the British Library.US Library of
Congress Cataloging-in-Publication
Data has been applied for.

NOTES

• American (Imperial plus US cups) and
metric measurements are included in
these recipes for convenience, however
it is important to work with one set of
measurements only and not alternate
between the two within a recipe.
• All spoon measures are level unless
otherwise specified.
• Ovens should be preheated to the
specified temperatures. If using a
fan-assisted oven, adjust temperatures
according to the manufacturer's
instructions.
• When a recipe calls for the grated
zest of citrus fruit, buy unwaxed fruit
and wash well before using. If you can
only find treated fruit, scrub well in
warm soapy water before using.

PICTURE CREDITS

Chapter opener illustrations:
Adobe stock/Happypictures

Additional photography:
Peter Cassidy: page 144.
Kate Whitaker: pages 61 and 102.
Clare Winfield: pages 44 and 103.

CONTENTS

INTRODUCTION

There are a wide variety of dishes that fall into the category of salad. Green salads, vegetable salads, as well as salads including pasta, pulses/legumes, grains, beans, meat, poultry, eggs, cheese and seafood. Generally served cold or at room temperature and very rarely hot.

Since antiquity the restorative green salad has been celebrated. The earliest salads were wild greens and herbs seasoned with salt. These were a tonic after a dull winter diet and there has been an evolution since those times to a more formal way of serving salads in European cuisine. Where, traditionally, salads are eaten at the beginning of the meal as a starter/appetizer or after the main course/entrée. As cuisine has evolved it is now perfectly acceptable to serve a selection of larger, room temperature salads as a main meal, served family style to be shared by all, something influenced by other cultures.

Most leafy vegetables can be eaten raw, including all varieties of lettuce, cress family, endives, cabbage, spinach, romaine, rocket/arugula and fresh herbs. Other vegetables, raw or cooked, such as tomatoes, onions, cucumbers, peppers, beetroot/beet and many more can be included. Dry bread roasted with a little garlic and olive oil, whether sourdough or pita breads, can also be tossed into the salad.

Vegetable salads may be marinated with a dressing, such as coleslaw, which gets better with time. Or super-fresh leafy salads, which work best just dressed before serving. A mixed salad of roasted vegetables, with leafy greens and some pulses/legumes or cheese transform the salad into a meal on its own.

This book includes five chapters of recipes that are versatile, light and substantial or somewhere in between. There are Classic salads – timeless favourites that you will make time and time again such as The Perfect Side Salad, Green Side Salad and Tomato & Onion Side Salad. Refreshing Salads such as a Classic Middle Eastern Salad, which makes a light and crunchy side dish alongside a selection of mezze (small plates) or simply a great lunchbox filler. Energizing salads such as my Miso Brown Rice Salad with Tofu & Ginger Dressing demonstrate simplicity at its best, it travels well and is as delicious on the day it's made as the following day. Nourishing salads such as Roasted Pumpkins, Winter Leaves, Pink Peppercorn Labne with Mint & Pistachio Dressing, can be served directly from the sheet pan where the cooking juices meld with the dressing and not a single drop is wasted.

Finally, I have included a chapter of Nurturing salads, which includes an impressive platter for sharing of Jamón, Peaches, Endives, Blue cheese & Olives, combining beauty and taste to create the perfect crowd-pleaser.

Salads can be so exciting as the combinations of flavours and textures are endless – whether classic or modern or even with a twist, a good salad will never disappoint!

ALL ABOUT LEAVES

LETTUCE

There are quite a few categories of lettuce, but for our purposes we will refer to four: butterhead, iceberg, romaine/cos and loose-leaf.

Butterhead This head of lettuce has silky smooth leaves, which make it a salad favourite. They are very delicate in nature and are generally sold with their roots still in tact in packaging. These are best dressed and eaten straight away as they wilt quickly. The best way to store them is loosely wrapped in damp paper towel and back in their own packaging.

Iceberg A sturdy head of lettuce that was developed in the 1940s to hold up during shipping. It has a great crunch to it and is the standard base for chopped and wedge salads. It stores well in it's own packaging in the fridge much longer than others do.

Romaine/Cos It has long leaves with sturdy, crunchy ribs and frilly edges. Its sturdiness means that it can also stand up to cooking, such as getting tossed on the grill for a quick char. It is used in the classic Caesar Salad (see page 23) and is a great vehicle for a creamy dressing.

Loose-leaf Has soft leaves and comes in a variety of colours, with some varieties – red leaf and green leaf – being named for their tint. Oak leaf, which also can be red or green, is another common variety that closely resembles red and green leaf lettuces. These are best stored unopened in their own packaging.

MESCLUN

Often refers to early/baby leaves and is traditionally what the French pick in early spring. In English, it is young salad greens or baby leaf and usually a mix of at least four types of leaves, such as rocket/arugula, endive/chicory, chervil, young red and green lettuces, baby spinach, mustard greens, frisée, mizuna, young Swiss chard, radicchio and sorrel. These are very tender and delicate and are best used straight away with a light acid-based dressing, such as a vinaigrette.

RADICCHIO

There are a few types of radicchio such as Chioggia, which is red and round and a mix of bitter and sweet; and Treviso, which is longer but less bitter than other varieties. There are also other heirloom varieties that are paler in colour with speckled red, which makes them much milder in flavour.

ENDIVE/CHICORY

Small and oval shaped, these leaves are known for having a juicy crunch. They can be either red or pale green, with the pale green having a milder bitterness. In addition to salads, the leaves of endive make a great addition to a crudité platter as they are perfect for scooping dips and spreads.

KALE & CAVALO NERO

A modern addition to salads, either raw and macerated in acid, or blanched and cooled and added. Remove the sturdy rib and give mature leaves a nice massage to tenderize them (baby kale leaves can be eaten whole). Curly is the most common variety of kale, but another type is cavalo nero, also known as Tuscan or dinosaur kale, which has dark, blue-green leaves.

ROCKET/ARUGULA

These tender leaves are known for their peppery bite. To the Romans, it was considered an aphrodisiac. It is wonderful in salads and pairs very well with balsamic vinegar. It wilts almost instantly when dressing touches it, so best to dress just before you serve.

SPINACH

When it comes to salads, baby spinach is the variety of choice as the larger spinach can be tough and fibrous and is better suited for cooking.

WATERCRESS

This is the oldest documented green and dates back to being used in Greece and Rome where, according to sources, it was fed to soldiers before battle. These leaves pack a peppery punch, but can have a fibrous stem, so consider removing part of it before adding.

OTHERS VARIETIES

Frisee means 'curly' in French, which makes sense when you see its frilly leaves. Curly endive is sometimes simply called 'chicory', and compared to curly endive, escarole has nice broad leaves that are less frilly. Sharply flavoured with a lingering bite, mustards are one of the more versatile greens because they can be eaten raw, dried and cooked.

CLEANING AND STORAGE

Lettuces such as iceberg and romaine should have decent heft to them to account for the water content. The crisper drawer in your fridge is the best option for storing. Heads of lettuce should be placed in a plastic or reusable produce bag and will last longer if kept whole.

Leaves are best kept loosely packed in a sealable container, which protects them from getting damaged. If keeping for an extended time, line the storage container with paper towel, then add the leaves on top, and layer with more towels and leaves, if storing a larger quantity.

For washing your greens, a big bowl of cold water is all you need. If washing headed lettuces, start by separating the leaves, then submerge the leaves in the cold water, gently swish them around with your hand, let them sit for anywhere from a few seconds to a few minutes, and then lift them out, leaving any dirt or grit behind. If you notice that the water is particularly murky, dump the water and repeat this process until sufficiently clean.

MAKING SALADS MORE SUBSTANTIAL

Transforming a salad from a side dish to a main is very easy. Take the classic Caesar Salad (see page 23), traditionally it uses boiled eggs and croûtons, but adding crispy bacon and some chicken really transforms it to a substantial salad, which becomes main worthy. There is a cornucopia of ingredients that you can add to make salads more hefty – some griddled halloumi, slow-roasted tomatoes, peppered mackerel, prawns/shrimps and a whole host more.

But how to put a proper salad together? There are a few rules, then the world is your oyster. It's all about experimenting with flavours and foods that you like.

1. *Start by choosing a base:* try mixed leafy greens, baby spinach, kale or rocket/arugula, or some super crunchy iceberg lettuce.

2. *Add some crunch:* beans, cauliflower, carrot, celery, cucumber, radish, sprouts or onion.

3. *Move onto your protein:* even if your salad is an accompaniment to a meal, there's still a place for protein. Try quinoa, buckwheat or toast up some chickpeas/garbanzo beans. Don't forget the odd egg either – a nice runny yolk makes an extra dressing.

4. *Add some fat:* good fats such as cheese (all sorts of cheese... including feta, Parmesan and goats' cheese), avocado, flaxseed oil, olive oil or tahini are delicious additions.

5. *A little bit more texture:* finish with tossing in some nuts or seeds. Add handfuls of herbs such as mint, coriander/cilantro or basil.

6. *For the dressing:* keep it simple or make the dressing a star. You can even just drizzle over a little quality olive oil. Keep an eye out for infused oils for extra flavour.

HOW TO DRESS A SALAD

A proper dressing is a mixture of a good oil with some acid, such as vinegar and or lemon, maybe some other flavour, such as mustard and finely chopped shallots, and salt and pepper. Dressings are elevated with salt and pepper. It truly is the secret to a great dressing. So you must taste it as you go along.

To master a good dressing you must understand the mother of all dressings, the basic French vinaigrette:

You will need:

2 tbsp good vinegar or 1 tbsp lemon juice

1 tsp Dijon or wholegrain mustard

pinch of sea salt

6 tbsp good oil

other flavours of choice

sea salt and freshly ground black pepper

Place the vinegar or lemon juice, mustard (to thicken and emulsify) and salt in a glass jar with a screw lid, then tighten the lid and shake vigorously. Add the oil. At this point you can add crushed garlic or finely chopped shallot, to suit your taste. Tighten the lid again and shake until it has thickened. Now, season to taste, which means... taste it, then add salt or vinegar or oil, shake it up and taste again.

Other salad dressings are derivatives on this basic salt/acid/oil formula with a world of substitutions available to you. Master this standard recipe and you will understand them all.

CREATE A PERFECTLY DRESSED SALAD

Most salads must be dressed in the moment, when the rest of the dinner is prepared, and people are ready to sit down to welcome it. Follow these simple steps to the perfect salad:

1. Prepare your dressing and all other toppings and set aside.

2. Put your prepared salad greens and herbs in a large mixing bowl.

3. Add half of your prepared dressing and toss lightly. Toss until the leaves are lightly coated and well mixed.

4. Taste; add more dressing if needed, a little at a time.

5. Gently place the salad onto a serving platter.

6. It's now time to add your toppings, some final cracked pepper and when you get to the table, finish with the remaining dressing.

GENERAL RULES

- Don't dress your salad too early.

- Simple is best.

- Salads aren't just for summer – there are absolutely lovely roasted vegetable salads that are finished with winter greens.

- Salads aren't just about leaves and vegetables so match the salad to the protein.

- Create contrasting flavours in your salad by using a variety of ingredients with different textures.

- Storing leafy greens: it's all about paper towels. Placing paper towels between layers of leaves to prevent browning, wilting and spoilage.

- If you plan to use a plastic bag for storage, be sure to press out any excess air. With a storage container, ensure that it's tightly sealed. Don't pack the leaves too tightly, or they won't have breathing room.

- Generally a dressed salad is best eaten on the day it's made, but I absolutely love placing the remnants of the salad bowl in the fridge and eating it straight from the bowl the next day and mopping up the juices with bread. So basically – rules can be broken... sometimes.

THE CLASSICS

WELL KNOWN & POPULAR SALADS, PERFECTED

SHARING PLATTER:
COBB SALAD

This American favourite, which is traditionally laid out in rows, works as a great main dish. The combination of crisp lettuce, charred corn, juicy chicken and salty bacon works so well together – it promises to become your favourite, too!

First, prepare the dressing. In a jar, shake together the vinegar, mustard, honey and oil and season with salt and pepper.

On a large platter, spread out the lettuce, then add rows of corn, egg, chicken, bacon, avocado, blue cheese and cherry tomatoes.

Season with salt and pepper, drizzle with the dressing and garnish with chives to serve.

1 romaine lettuce, roughly chopped

2 charred corn-on-the-cobs, kernels removed

4 x 6-minute boiled eggs, peeled and quartered

300 g/10½ oz. cooked chicken, roughly chopped

8 slices of bacon, cooked and crumbled

1 avocado, peeled, stoned/pitted and thinly sliced

100 g/3½ oz. blue cheese, crumbled

300 g/2 cups cherry tomatoes, halved

sea salt and freshly ground black pepper

2 tbsp finely chopped chives, to garnish

DRESSING

4 tbsp red wine vinegar

1 tbsp Dijon mustard

½ tsp honey

8 tbsp extra virgin olive oil

SERVES 4

SALADE RACHEL

The French do make the most amazing salads. Salade Rachel originates from the region of Gironde and is a combination of celery, shaved truffles, artichokes, boiled potatoes, asparagus and mayonnaise. In my version, the truffle has been mixed into the mayonnaise dressing.

Start by boiling a large saucepan of water and blanching the celery sticks for a few minutes, then refresh them in iced water. Keep the water boiling and blanch, then refresh the asparagus.

Put the lemon juice, truffles in olive oil, mayonnaise and some salt and pepper in the base of a serving dish and mix together.

Thinly slice the blanched celery and add it to the serving dish on top of the truffle mayo mixture, followed by the new potatoes, asparagus tips and frisée lettuce. Finish with a drizzle of olive oil and serve with a glass of crisp white wine.

½ head of celery, leaves picked and reserved

bunch of asparagus tips

freshly squeezed juice of 1 lemon

1 tbsp truffles preserved in olive oil (or a few shavings of fresh summer truffle)

3 tbsp mayonnaise

200 g/7 oz. new potatoes, boiled and cooled

1 frisée lettuce, leaves picked

sea salt and freshly ground black pepper

drizzle of olive oil, to serve

SERVES 2

SALADE DE CAROTTES

This vibrant and refreshing carrot salad is a classic in France. Grated carrots are tossed with lemon juice, olive oil, mustard, honey, seasoning and some fresh herbs. The carrots can be finely or coarsely grated, depending on your preference.

Stir together the olive oil, lemon juice, mustard, honey and a little salt in a mixing bowl. Add the carrots and chopped herbs and toss thoroughly with the dressing.

Taste, and season with additional lemon juice and salt and pepper if needed.

2 tbsp extra virgin olive oil

freshly squeezed juice of ½ lemon, or more to taste

1 tsp mustard

½ tsp runny honey

450 g/1 lb. carrots, peeled and grated

2 tbsp finely chopped mixed fresh herbs (parsley, tarragon, chives or chervil)

sea salt and freshly ground black pepper

SERVES 2

THE PERFECT SIDE SALAD

What constitutes the perfect side salad? Something that goes with everything? A very hard taskmaster and these two salads fit the bill. The dressings and herb additions can be tweaked to suit the main meal.

GREEN SIDE SALAD

This must be crisp and well dressed. Dress just before you serve or even dress the salad at the table. The addition of tarragon with its light liquorice taste is a perfect side to a classic meal. Alternatively, change up the herbs to parsley and chervil for a cleansing side salad or even add mint into the salad and serve on the side of roast lamb.

Rinse the lettuce and put it in a bowl with very cold water to give a little extra crispness.

Meanwhile, mix the shallot, vinegar and the mustards in a small bowl to combine, then, while stirring, slowly add the olive oil. Season to taste.

Drain the lettuce well, add the spinach, rocket and herbs and drizzle with the vinaigrette to taste. Toss to combine and serve.

1 cos lettuce, leaves separated

100 g/2 cups baby spinach and rocket/arugula

2 tbsp finely chopped chives

2 fresh tarragon sprigs, leaves picked (optional)

DRESSING

1 shallot, very finely chopped

3 tbsp white wine vinegar

1 tsp Dijon mustard

1 tsp wholegrain mustard

6 tbsp olive oil

sea salt and freshly ground black pepper

SERVES 4

TOMATO & ONION SIDE SALAD

This juicy, crunchy and fragrant salad is a simple way to add a refreshing side dish to spicy mains or slow-cooked meats.

Place the onion with a pinch of salt, the lime juice and zest, olive oil, honey and chilli flakes in a bowl and leave to sit for 30 minutes.

Meanwhile, chop the cherry tomatoes and place in the bowl with all the juices and mix well. Finish with the herbs and toss to combine.

Note you can change the herbs depending on what you are serving this salad with or just use one type of herb rather than a mixture.

½ onion, finely diced

grated zest and juice of 1 lime

3 tbsp olive oil

1 tsp runny honey

½ tsp dried chilli/hot red pepper flakes (optional)

400 g/2 cups cherry tomatoes

3 tbsp mixed fresh parsley, coriander/cilantro and mint

sea salt

SERVES 4

CAESAR SALAD

This is a heartily substantial and delicious classic salad. An overdressed Caesar can be overwhelming, so a light coating of dressing is best and then place extra dressing on the table for people to serve themselves. You may be left with extra dressing but it keeps for a week in the fridge and works great with griddled chicken and lettuce as an alternative meal.

Preheat the oven to 190°C/170°C fan/375°F/Gas 5.

First, prepare the dressing. Place the eggs in a large heatproof bowl, cover completely with boiling water and leave to stand for about 15 minutes until coddled. This ensures that you are not using completely raw yolks for the dressing. Drain, then briefly refresh under cold running water. Peel, then transfer the yolks to a food processor, discarding the whites and shells.

Add the lemon juice, anchovies, garlic and Worcestershire sauce and process to combine. With the motor running, add the oil in a thin steady stream until emulsified. Season to taste, then stir through the Parmesan and set aside.

For the garlic croûtons, brush the baguette slices with oil and place them on a baking sheet. Bake in the preheated oven for 8–12 minutes, turning once, until golden and crisp. Remove from the oven, then rub with the cut side of the garlic cloves.

Meanwhile, scatter cos leaves over a serving platter, drizzle with the dressing, scatter over the eggs and bacon, if using, plus some extra Parmesan and anchovies. Top with the garlic croûtons to serve.

1 cos lettuce, leaves separated and chopped

4 x 6-minute boiled eggs, peeled and quartered

8 slices of smoked streaky bacon, cooked until crispy (optional)

CAESAR DRESSING

4 eggs, at room temperature

60 ml/¼ cup fresh lemon juice

2–4 anchovy fillets, plus extra to serve (depending on taste)

1–2 garlic cloves, crushed

1 tsp Worcestershire sauce

125 ml/½ cup olive oil

50 g/⅔ cup finely grated Parmesan, plus extra to serve

GARLIC CROÛTONS

½ day-old sourdough baguette, thinly sliced

100 ml/scant ½ cup olive oil

3 garlic cloves, halved

SERVES 4

WALDORF SALAD

This is a timeless salad, one that has stood the test of time. Originally it was just four ingredients but this recipe is an evolved version, which is not far off the original. Mixing the mayonnaise with Greek yogurt adds a tang to the dressing and a lightness for a modern touch.

First, make the mayonnaise. Blend the egg yolk, vinegar and mustard in a food processor until well combined. Mix the two oils in a measuring jug/pitcher. With the motor running, add the combined oils in a thin steady stream, then add the lemon juice and zest and some salt and pepper to taste.

Preheat the oven to 200°C/180°C fan/400°F/Gas 6.

Spread the walnuts out on a baking sheet and toast in the preheated oven until golden. Set aside to cool.

Cut the unpeeled apples into julienne and combine with half the lemon juice in a bowl. Add the walnuts, celery, endives, grapes and parsley.

Make the dressing by mixing the mayonnaise, Greek yogurt, a drizzle of walnut oil and the reserved lemon juice together in a bowl.

Place the lettuce on a platter or a shallow bowl, then top with the apple and walnut mixture and season to taste. Scatter with celery leaves and extra walnuts, drizzle over the dressing and serve immediately.

75 g/½ cup walnuts, plus extra to serve

2 Granny Smith apples

juice of 1 lemon

½ bunch of celery, finely sliced widthways, heart leaves reserved for serving

2 endives/chicory, leaves separated

200 g/1½ cups red seedless grapes

30 g/1 cup fresh parsley, leaves picked

½ butter lettuce, leaves separated

MAYONNAISE

1 egg yolk

1 tbsp white wine vinegar

1 tsp Dijon mustard

60 ml/¼ cup olive oil

25 ml/1½ tbsp walnut oil

grated zest and juice of ½ lemon

sea salt and freshly ground black pepper

DRESSING

2 tbsp mayonnaise (see above)

2 tbsp Greek yogurt

extra drizzle of walnut oil

SERVES 4

PANZANELLA

The simplest, most delicious salad originating from Tuscany, using tomato-soaked bread, roasted red (bell) peppers and fresh basil. This is best served in the season for ripe tomatoes for the tastiest version of this salad.

Preheat the oven to 220°C/200°C fan/425°F/Gas 7.

Place the peppers in a roasting pan, drizzle with a little olive oil and roast in the preheated oven for about 30–35 minutes, turning occasionally, until browned and the skins have blistered.

Transfer to a bowl, cover with clingfilm/plastic wrap and leave to stand and steam. Peel the peppers, tear into coarse pieces and set aside.

Meanwhile, combine the tomatoes and sugar in a large bowl, season to taste and leave to stand for about 30 minutes until juicy.

Add the bread, extra virgin olive oil, vinegar, onion and garlic to the tomatoes. Toss to combine and leave for 30 minutes for the flavours to develop.

Add the roast peppers and basil, toss to combine and adjust the seasoning to taste. Serve with a wedge of pecorino topped with a drizzle of honey and some olives.

4 red romano peppers

olive oil, for drizzling

650 g/1 lb. 7 oz. mixed baby tomatoes, large ones quartered, smaller ones halved

200 g/7 oz. mixed tomatoes, coarsely chopped

½ tsp caster/granulated sugar

300 g/11½ oz. sourdough, coarsely torn

100 ml/scant ½ cup extra virgin olive oil

60 ml/¼ cup aged red wine vinegar

1 red onion, thinly sliced

1 garlic clove, finely crushed

30 g/1 cup fresh basil, leaves picked

sea salt and freshly ground black pepper

pecorino, green olives and runny honey, to serve

SERVES 4

COLESLAW
4 WAYS

MAYO SLAW

This is inspired by my mother in-law who makes this time and time again, either on Boxing Day or for a summer barbecue or picnic. My version has more herbs in it. It is a family favourite and can be eaten for a few days.

Place the cabbage, carrots, red pepper, apple, red onions, radishes, mixed herbs, raisins and peanuts in a bowl and set aside.

Meanwhile, in a jug/pitcher, mix the mustard, mayonnaise, yogurt, sugar and vinegar. Season well and taste for sharpness and creamy. Add more vinegar if needed.

Pour the dressing onto the cabbage mixture, mix well and finish with a few pinches of paprika.

1 small white cabbage, shredded

2 carrots, grated

1 red (bell) pepper, deseeded and thinly sliced

1 apple, grated

1 red onion, thinly sliced

5 radishes, thinly sliced

½ small bunch fresh dill, chives, parsley or coriander/cilantro, finely chopped

50 g/⅓ cup raisins

50 g/⅓ cup salted peanuts

DRESSING

1 tbsp wholegrain mustard

100 g/scant ½ cup mayonnaise

50 g/scant ¼ cup yogurt

½ tsp caster/granulated sugar

1–2 tbsp white wine vinegar

a few pinches of paprika

sea salt and freshly ground black pepper

SERVES 4

ASIAN SLAW

This crispy Asian-influenced slaw is the perfect side for meat and fish dishes.

Place the cabbage, carrots, spring onions and herbs in a large mixing bowl and toss together. Mix together the ingredients for the dressing and toss the dressing through the slaw just before serving. Top with crispy shallots, if using.

¼ Asian cabbage, thinly sliced

2 small carrots, grated

2 spring onions/scallions, thinly sliced on the diagonal

a handful of fresh coriander/cilantro

a handful of Thai basil

crispy fried shallots, to serve (optional)

DRESSING

2 tbsp rice vinegar

2 tbsp sweet chilli/chili sauce

1 tbsp fish sauce

SERVES 6

RAINBOW SLAW

A colourful slaw-style salad to brighten up any plate. It's an ideal winter slaw to serve as part of your festive menu too.

Place all the dressing ingredients with the herbs in a serving dish and give it a good stir.

Add all the other ingredients to the serving dish, season with salt and pepper and toss to combine. Serve immediately.

¼ white cabbage, finely shredded

½ purple cabbage, finely shredded

100 g/1 cup Brussels sprouts, thinly sliced

1 carrot, grated

1 small red onion, thinly sliced

2 tbsp pumpkin seeds, toasted

sea salt and freshly ground black pepper

HERB DRESSING

100 ml/⅓ cup extra virgin olive oil

juice of 1 lemon

1 tbsp apple cider vinegar

1 tsp runny honey

1 tsp Dijon mustard

a small bunch of fresh parsley, finely chopped

½ small bunch of fresh chives, finely chopped

2 sprigs of fresh tarragon, finely chopped

SERVES 6

CABBAGE, APPLE & CELERY SLAW

The crispy bite of cabbage and celery pairs perfectly with the sweet apple, which is all enhanced by a herby, zingy dressing.

For the dressing, combine all the ingredients in a small bowl, whisk to combine and season to taste with salt and pepper. Set aside.

Place the slaw ingredients in a large serving bowl and toss to combine.

Pour the dressing over, then toss gently to mix and serve immediately.

200 g/7 oz. white cabbage, core removed, finely shredded

200 g/7 oz. red cabbage, core removed, finely shredded

1 red onion, halved and thinly sliced

1 celery heart, base thinly sliced, stalks/ribs thinly sliced lengthways and placed in iced water, leaves reserved

1 Granny Smith apple, cored and cut into julienne

PARSLEY & APPLE CIDER DRESSING

80 ml/⅓ cup apple cider vinegar

60 ml/¼ cup apple juice

1 tsp maple syrup

2 tbsp extra virgin olive oil

3 tbsp freshly squeezed lemon juice

½ bunch fresh parsley, finely chopped

2 sprigs fresh tarragon, leaves picked and finely chopped

½ bunch fresh chives, chopped

sea salt and freshly ground black pepper

SERVES 4

BEAN SALAD
3 WAYS

CANNELLINI BEAN SALAD

This salad is so adaptable – it can easily become a hearty salad with the addition of sautéed chorizo and rocket/arugula, but is just as nice in its simplicity with the sharp dressing and parsley.

Drain the beans and set aside. Place all the other ingredients in a serving bowl and whisk. Add the beans and serve.

400 g/14-oz. can cannellini beans

2 shallots, finely chopped

½ tbsp sherry vinegar

juice of ½ lemon

4 tbsp olive oil

a handful of fresh flat-leaf parsley, roughly chopped

sea salt and freshly ground black pepper

SERVES 6 AS AN APPETIZER

GREEN BEAN, POTATO & PESTO SALAD

Some classic tastes here combine to make a satisfying salad.

Bring a large saucepan of salted water to the boil, add the green beans and cook for 5–6 minutes or until just tender. Using a slotted spoon, transfer to a colander and refresh under cold running water.

Place the potatoes in a saucepan, cover with cold, salted water and simmer over a medium heat for 15 minutes or until tender. Drain, cool slightly, peel and quarter.

For the pesto, combine the basil leaves, garlic and a pinch of sea salt in a mortar and, using a pestle, coarsely crush. Add the pine nuts and Parmesan and pound to a smooth paste. Stir the lemon juice and zest and oil through and season to taste with salt and black pepper.

In a large bowl, combine the beans and potatoes, season to taste and serve drizzled with the pesto and some extra-virgin olive oil.

500 g/1 lb. 2 oz. mixed green beans

500 g/1 lb. 2 oz. baby new potatoes

PESTO

75 g/2 cups fresh basil leaves

3 garlic cloves, peeled

50 g/⅓ cup pine nuts, toasted

100 g/3½ oz. Parmesan, grated

grated zest and juice of 1 lemon (or to taste)

80 ml/⅓ cup extra virgin olive oil, plus extra to serve

sea salt and freshly ground black pepper

SERVES 4 AS A SIDE

BRAISED BUTTER
BEAN SALAD

The most humble and elegant side or salad that you will make time and time again. It can be served just warm, or at room temperature and the next day it will taste even better.

Combine the beans, stock, oil and lemon peel in a saucepan and bring to the boil. Reduce the heat to medium and simmer until the beans are softened and the stock has reduced by two-thirds.

Remove from the heat, stir in the sliced celery and olives and leave to cool to room temperature.

Toss the bean mixture with the herbs and celery leaves in a bowl, season to taste and serve drizzled with olive oil.

400 g/14 oz. canned butter/lima beans, drained

200 ml/scant 1 cup vegetable stock

50 ml/scant ¼ cup extra-virgin olive oil, plus extra to serve

3 lemon peels

2 celery stalks/ribs, peeled and thinly sliced, plus pale leaves to serve

100 g/1 cup green olives, stoned/pitted and crushed

1 tbsp freshly chopped mint

1 tbsp freshly chopped flat-leaf parsley

fresh dill sprigs, to garnish

SERVES 4 AS A SIDE

PASTA SALAD FOR A BBQ

This substantial salad works perfectly as a side dish for a barbecue or large gathering. A little goes a long way, and the tastes combine beautifully when paired with grilled meats.

Cook the orecchiette in a large saucepan of salted boiling water until al dente. Drain the pasta in a colander, then set aside to drain while you make the dressing.

In a serving dish, whisk the lemon juice, shallot, maple syrup and mustard. Whisking constantly, slowly drizzle in the olive oil until the mixture is emulsified. Season with salt and pepper.

In a large bowl, combine the pasta, spinach and rocket, edamame, peas and broad beans, cucumbers, spring onions, herbs, jalapeños, capers and lemon zest. Toss together for 1–2 minutes, until the spinach and rocket have reduced in volume and becomes slightly wilted.

Add the artichoke hearts and pumpkin seeds and toss gently until just combined.

Season to taste with salt, pepper, chilli flakes and pecorino, if using.

200 g/7 oz. orecchiette

50 g/2 cups mixed spinach and rocket/arugula

120 g/1 cup mixed edamame beans, petit pois and broad beans

2 small cucumbers, quartered lengthways and chopped

3 spring onions/scallions, finely sliced

10 g/⅓ cup fresh flat-leaf parsley, roughly chopped

10 g/⅓ cup fresh mint, leaves picked and chopped

2 jalapeños, thinly sliced into rounds

3 tbsp capers, drained

grated zest of 1 lemon

100 g/3½ oz. artichoke hearts

50 g/⅓ cup pumpkin seeds, toasted

½ tsp dried chilli/hot red pepper flakes (optional)

freshly grated pecorino, to garnish (optional)

DRESSING

juice of 1 lemon

1 shallot, finely chopped

1 tsp maple syrup

1 tsp wholegrain mustard

80 ml/⅓ cup extra virgin olive oil

sea salt and freshly ground black pepper

SERVES 4

SALADE NIÇOISE

This French classic is a great salad to serve at an informal lunch or even as a first course. It can be bulked up by adding some rocket/ arugula, a baguette on the side and a crisp glass of white wine. There are so many versions of this that include charred tuna steak, which can easily be added instead of the canned tuna. Be sure to use a nice quality tuna for extra luxury.

First, make the dressing. In a pestle and mortar, crush the flakes of sea salt to a powder, then add the garlic clove and pound them into a smooth paste. Add the mustard and work that in, then add the vinegar and some freshly milled black pepper. Mix thoroughly until the salt dissolves. Add the olive oil and mix together. Now stir the herbs into the vinaigrette. Just before you dress the salad, pour everything into a screw-top jar and shake vigorously so it's thoroughly blended.

Cut each tomato into quarters and arrange them in a large salad bowl with the cucumber, potatoes, beans and chopped shallots in layers, sprinkling a little of the dressing in as you go.

Arrange chunks of tuna and egg quarters on top, then add the anchovies, followed by a scattering of olives, and a final sprinkling of dressing to finish.

Serve with a crusty baguette and lovely butter.

350 g/12½ oz. tomatoes

1 cucumber, cut into half moons

450 g/1 lb. baby new potatoes, cooked and sliced

150 g/5½ oz. green beans, cooked and halved diagonally

4 shallots, peeled and thinly sliced

2 x 200 g/7 oz. cans tuna (good quality)

4 x 6-minute boiled eggs, peeled and quartered

50 g/1¾ oz. anchovy fillets

100 g/1 cup small stoned/ pitted black olives (preferably French)

crusty baguette and butter, to serve

DRESSING

1 tsp sea salt

1 garlic clove, peeled and left whole

1 tsp Dijon mustard

1 tbsp white wine vinegar

6 tbsp olive oil

1 tbsp freshly chopped herbs (chervil, chives, parsley and basil)

freshly ground black pepper

SERVES 4

POTATO SALAD
3 WAYS

SIMPLE POTATO SALAD

This is the type of potato salad I grew up eating in my Greek family household. The key with this salad is that you dress it when the potatoes are still warm. The dressing will infuse the potatoes for a lovely side.

Rinse and scrub the potatoes, then slice into halves depending how big they are. Add to a large saucepan and cover with water. Place over a high heat and bring to the boil. Reduce the heat slightly and continue cooking for 10–15 minutes or until the potatoes are easily pierced with a knife and also easily slide off the knife. Drain. Once the potatoes are mostly dry, add them to a large serving bowl. Season with a dash of salt and black pepper and apple cider vinegar. Set aside.

Meanwhile, prepare the dressing. Add the mustard, garlic, salt, pepper, white wine vinegar and apple cider vinegar to a mixing bowl and whisk to combine. While continuing to whisk, slowly stream in the olive oil to emulsify the oil and vinegar. Add the dill and whisk once more. Taste and adjust the flavour as needed.

Add the dressing to the potatoes, along with the spring onions and parsley, and toss to combine. Serve warm, chilled or at room temperature – that's the beauty of this salad.

1 kg/2¼ lb. baby potatoes, scrubbed

4 spring onions/scallions, finely sliced

2 tbsp freshly chopped parsley

sea salt and freshly ground black pepper

DRESSING

2 tbsp wholegrain mustard

1 garlic clove, crushed

2 tbsp white wine vinegar

1 tbsp apple cider vinegar

4 tbsp extra virgin olive oil

2 tbsp freshly chopped dill

SERVES 4

CLASSIC MAYO POTATO SALAD

Always a crowd pleaser and perfect for serving alongside grilled sausages.

Cook the potatoes in a saucepan of boiling salted water until tender, then drain and set aside to steam dry.

Combine the remaining ingredients in a bowl and season to taste.

Add the potatoes and gently mix to coat well, then transfer to a serving platter. Scatter with extra parsley, season with black pepper and serve.

6 large potatoes, cut into 5-cm/2-in. cubes

250 g/1 cup crème fraîche

150 g/⅔ cup mayonnaise

1 tsp Dijon mustard

1 tbsp white wine vinegar

70 g/scant ½ cup baby capers, drained

100 g/3½ oz. cornichons, thinly sliced

2 shallots, peeled and thinly sliced

2 tbsp freshly chopped chives

1 tbsp freshly chopped flat-leaf parsley, plus extra to serve

freshly ground black pepper

SERVES 4

ROAST POTATO SALAD

This is a hybrid salad and side and my favourite way to eat a salad. Mixed with roasted, fresh and well-dressed components. This is lovely just warm or room temperature and can be made in advance. Perfect when cooking for a crowd.

Preheat the oven to 220°C/200°C fan/425°F/Gas 7.

Toss the potatoes in the olive oil, season with salt and pepper and roast for 20 minutes. Add the radishes, mixing them through the potatoes and cook for a final 5 minutes until cooked through.

For the dressing, melt the butter and olive oil in a frying pan/skillet over a medium heat, then stir in the garlic and lemon zest. Remove from the heat, whisk in the mustard and lemon juice, season to taste, then pour the dressing over the roasted potatoes and radishes.

Serve the salad warm, scattered with wild leaves, dill, spring onions and goat's cheese, if using.

500 g/1 lb. 2 oz. small new potatoes, scrubbed, halved

2 tbsp olive oil

200 g/7 oz. radishes, halved if large

150 g/5½ oz. mixed wild leaves, such as nasturtiums and watercress

20 g/⅔ cup fresh dill, roughly chopped (or to taste)

4 spring onions/scallions, thinly sliced into rounds

60 g/2 oz. soft goat's cheese, crumbled (optional)

sea salt and freshly ground black pepper

WARM LEMON GARLIC DRESSING

30 g/2 tbsp butter, coarsely chopped

30 ml/2 tbsp extra virgin olive oil

2 garlic cloves, finely chopped

grated zest and juice of 1 lemon

1 tsp Dijon mustard

SERVES 4

GREEK SALAD

There are so many incarnations of this salad and each region
in Greece has a slightly different way of serving it. This is by far
my favourite way. Traditionally, it's finished with dried oregano
but if you can get fresh oregano it's a nice change.

Toss the onion and salt in a bowl and leave to stand for 10 minutes. Add
the vinegar and leave to stand for another 10 minutes until softened.

Combine the red pepper, tomato, cucumber, olives and radishes in
a serving bowl. Scatter with the onion and dress with the oil and the
vinegar from the onion mixture.

Season to taste, top with feta and sprinkle with oregano to serve.

½ red onion, thinly sliced

½ tsp salt

100 ml/scant ½ cup red wine
vinegar

1 red (bell) pepper, sliced

3 ripe tomatoes, cut into
wedges

1 large cucumber or 4 small
ones, cut into wedges

10 Kalamata olives, stoned/
pitted

10 radishes, quartered

4 tbsp extra virgin olive oil

150 g/5½ oz. piece of Greek
feta, crumbled

1 tsp dried Greek oregano or
3–4 fresh oregano sprigs

SERVES 4

SHREDDED CHICKEN SALAD
3 WAYS

CRUNCHY VIETNAMESE CHICKEN SALAD

A super crunchy, zingy salad that is perfect to feed a crowd. Frying the shallots adds an element of depth to this fresh salad, but you can buy crispy onions and use those instead if preferred.

In a small bowl, combine all the dressing ingredients along with 1 tablespoon water and stir until the sugar is dissolved. Allow the dressing to stand for 5 minutes.

Meanwhile, in a small saucepan, heat the vegetable oil until shimmering. Add the shallots and cook over a high heat, stirring constantly, for about 3–4 minutes until golden. Drain the shallots on paper towels; reserve the oil for another use. Sprinkle the shallots with salt and let cool.

In a large bowl, toss the cabbage, carrots, red onion, coriander, mint and shredded chicken. Add the olive oil and the dressing and toss everything together well. Sprinkle with the peanuts and fried shallots and serve the chicken salad with lime wedges.

250 ml/1 cup vegetable oil, for frying

2 large shallots, thinly sliced

½ small head cabbage, finely shredded

2 carrots, finely grated

1 red onion, thinly sliced

30 g/1 cup fresh coriander/ cilantro, leaves picked

30 g/1 cup fresh mint, leaves picked

400 g/14 oz. roasted chicken, shredded

2 tbsp extra-virgin olive oil

3 tbsp dry roasted peanuts

sea salt

lime wedges, to serve

DRESSING

2 tbsp palm sugar (or light brown sugar)

2½ tbsp fish sauce

1½ tbsp lime juice

1½ tbsp rice vinegar

1 birds eye chilli/chile, thinly sliced

1 garlic clove, crushed

SERVES 4

FRESH & LIGHT CORONATION CHICKEN SALAD

A lighter version of the original by using a lighter mayonnaise and yogurt or crème fraîche in the dressing. The shredded chicken could easily be replaced by cooked turkey for a Boxing Day salad.

In a small bowl, mix together the yogurt, mayonnaise, chutney and curry powder. Season and add lime juice and zest to taste. Set aside.

In a large bowl, toss together the mango, spring onions and chicken. Add three-quarters of the dressing and gently toss to coat.

Place the salad leaves in a bowl and drizzle with a little olive oil and a squeeze of lime juice. Season with a little salt and pepper, toss to coat and divide between serving plates. Serve the chicken salad on top.

Add a little water or olive oil to the remaining dressing to loosen if needed, mix well and then drizzle over the salad. Scatter with the toasted almonds, coriander and sliced green chilli, if using.

50 g/¼ cup Greek yogurt or crème fraiche

50 g/¼ cup mayonnaise (lighter)

1 tbsp mango chutney

2 tsp medium curry powder

grated zest and juice of 1 lime

1 mango, stoned/pitted and sliced

2 spring onions/scallions, trimmed and thinly sliced

400 g/14 oz. roasted/ cooked chicken, skinless and shredded

small bag of watercress

small bag of baby spinach leaves

sea salt and freshly ground black pepper

extra virgin olive oil, for drizzling

TO SERVE

2 tbsp flaked/slivered almonds, toasted

1 tbsp freshly chopped coriander/cilantro

green chilli/chile, sliced into rounds (optional)

SERVES 4

SUPERFOOD CHICKEN SALAD

Green and full of goodness, this salad is the perfect salad to meal prep for the week. Just simply keep the dressing separate and drizzle when you serve.

Preheat the oven to 220°C/200°C fan/425°F/gas 7.

Place the sweet potatoes in a roasting tray with the chilli flakes, ground coriander and cinnamon, a drizzle of olive oil and a little sea salt and black pepper, then toss well. Spread out into an even layer and bake in the hot oven for 15–20 minutes, or until golden and crisp.

Meanwhile, cook the quinoa in a saucepan of boiling salted water according to the packet instructions.

In a separate pan of boiling water, blanch and refresh the tenderstem broccoli and cavalo nero and set aside.

Once cooked, drain and rinse the quinoa under cold running water, then leave to cool along with the broccoli. Remove the sweet potato from the oven and leave it to cool, too.

Meanwhile, toast the almonds in a dry frying pan/skillet over a medium-high heat for 2–3 minutes, then transfer to a pestle and mortar and crush lightly.

Halve the pomegranate and squeeze half the juice into a large bowl. Add 3 times as much extra virgin olive oil, the lemon juice, zest and pomegranate molasses. Whisk well and season to taste.

Add the cooled broccoli and cavalo nero to the dressing, then add the spinach leaves. Add the parsley (stalks and all) and chilli to the bowl along with the quinoa, sweet potato and chicken. Finish with the remaining pomegranate seeds.

1 sweet potato, chopped into 2.5-cm/1-in. chunks

pinch of dried chilli/hot red pepper flakes

pinch of ground coriander

small pinch of ground cinnamon

olive oil, for drizzling

300 g/11½ oz. roast chicken, shredded

200 g/7 oz. quinoa

200 g/7 oz. tenderstem broccoli

100 g/3½ oz. cavalo nero, roughly cut

20 g/4 tsp sesame seeds

50 g/⅓ cup raw almonds, chopped

1 pomegranate

extra virgin olive oil (see method for amount)

grated zest and juice of 1 lemon

1 tbsp pomegranate molasses

handful of baby spinach leaves

30 g/1 cup fresh parsley, roughly chopped

1 fresh red chilli/chile, finely sliced

sea salt and freshly ground black pepper

SERVES 2

SPRING GREENS SALAD WITH FETA & MINT DRESSING

This salad is so versatile and I guarantee it will become a regular. For a more substantial salad you can add some poached chicken. Additionally, you could also halve the lettuce and lightly char in a ridged stovetop griddle pan, just to add more taste but not to cook through. Or simply serve this as is.

For the feta dressing, shake the oil, lemon juice, vinegar and garlic in a screwtop jar or small bowl to combine. Season to taste, add the feta and refrigerate until needed.

Blanch the sugarsnap peas and beans in a pan of boiling water until bright green and just tender. Drain, refresh in iced water, then drain well and toss in a bowl with the cucumber and lettuce. Store in an airtight container until required.

To serve, add the mint to the dressing and then toss with the greens in a serving bowl.

150 g/5½ oz. sugarsnap peas, trimmed

150 g/5½ oz. green beans, trimmed and coarsely chopped

2 cucumbers, coarsely chopped

1 cos lettuce, coarsely chopped

FETA DRESSING

100 ml/generous ⅓ cup extra virgin olive oil

freshly squeezed juice of 1 lemon, or to taste

1 tbsp sherry vinegar

1 garlic clove, finely grated

100 g/3½ oz. feta, crumbled

½ bunch of mint, leaves torn

SERVES 4 AS A SIDE

SPINACH SALAD WITH HOT BACON DRESSING

Fresh robust green leaves served with a hot creamy dressing makes a perfect accompaniment to roast chicken or simply add roast chicken to make for a more substantial salad.

First, make the dressing. In a sauté pan, heat the oil over a medium–high heat. Add the bacon and cook until half crisp, darker in colour and the fat has released into the pan. Add the garlic, chilli flakes and bay leaf and toast until the mixture smells really fragrant and the garlic starts to turn golden brown. Add the shallots and cook until translucent.

Stir in the vinegar and sugar and cook for 4–5 minutes over a medium heat, scraping the base of the pan to release anything that's stuck. Season generously with salt and pepper. Add the cream and bring to the boil, then remove from heat. Add the thyme, leave to stand for 15 minutes, then discard the thyme.

Meanwhile, wash and thoroughly dry all the greens and combine in a mixing bowl.

Add the lemon zest and juice to the dressing and ladle the hot bacon dressing over the salad. The greens will slightly wilt and the dressing will coat all the leaves.

200 g/4 cups baby spinach leaves

10 watercress sprigs, trimmed

30 g/⅓ cup pea shoots

HOT BACON DRESSING

1 tsp flavourless oil

100 g/3½ oz. bacon lardons

2 garlic cloves, crushed

1 tsp dried chilli/hot red pepper flakes (or to taste)

1 fresh bay leaf

2 shallots, peeled and thinly sliced

1 tbsp white wine vinegar

1–2 tsp caster/granulated sugar

200 ml/scant 1 cup double/heavy cream

3 fresh thyme sprigs, plus extra to garnish

grated zest and juice of 1 lemon

sea salt and freshly ground black pepper

SERVES 4

CHEF'S SALAD FROM THE RITZ CARLTON

It is believed that the chef's salad was created in the 1940s by Louis Diat, a chef at the Ritz-Carlton Hotel in New York City. It started as an off-menu item where the chef would add cuts of deli meat, cheese and hard-boiled egg to the hotel's house salad.

First make the dressing. Put the ketchup, vinegar, sugar, Dijon mustard, paprika, white pepper and egg yolk into a bowl and whisk well. Slowly drizzle in the olive oil, whisking constantly, until smooth. Season with salt, then set the dressing aside.

Spread the salad leaves out on a salad plate. Arrange the ham, beef tongue, chicken, cheese and egg on top of the greens. Tuck the watercress into the centre and drizzle over some of the dressing to finish.

300 g/11½ oz. mixed salad leaves (more robust than soft and tender)

150 g/5½ oz. smoked ham, thinly sliced

50 g/1¾ oz. cooked beef tongue (optional)

150 g/5½ oz. cooked chicken breast, thinly sliced

30 g/1 oz. cheese, such as Cheddar, Parmesan (whatever you have in the fridge), thinly sliced or shaved

2 x 6-minute boiled eggs, cooled, peeled and quartered

30 g/½ cup watercress, trimmed

DRESSING

3 tbsp ketchup

3 tbsp red wine vinegar

1 tbsp caster/granulated sugar

1 tsp Dijion mustard

1 tsp sweet paprika

½ tsp ground white pepper

1 egg yolk

200 ml/ 1 scant cup extra virgin olive oil

sea salt

SERVES 2

LEON SALAD
FROM LA SCALA

This salad is a classic salad from the Los Angeles institution La Scala. Eaten by all sorts of celebrities and favoured by the Kardashians. The lettuce in this salad is best thinly sliced for the dressing to really coat the leaves. It will become a favourite in your home.

Place the iceberg lettuce, romaine, chickpeas, salami and mozzarella in a large salad bowl. Set it aside.

To make the dressing, whisk together the olive oil, red wine vinegar, mustard, salt and pepper in a measuring cup or a small bowl. Stir in the grated Parmesan.

Gently dress and toss the salad and serve with extra Parmesan on top.

1 iceberg lettuce, sliced

1 romaine lettuce, sliced

1 x 400 g/14 oz. canned chickpeas/garbanzo beans, rinsed and drained

120 g/4½ oz. Italian salami, julienned

100 g/3½ oz. mozzarella, grated

30 g/1 cup fresh parsley, roughly chopped

DRESSING

80 ml/⅓ cup extra virgin olive oil

2 tbsp red wine vinegar

2 tsp Dijon mustard

100 g/1 cup grated Parmesan cheese, plus extra to garnish

sea salt and freshly ground black pepper

SERVES 2

REFRESHING

LIGHT & BRIGHT, REMINISCENT OF A MEDITERRANEAN SUMMER

SHARING PLATTER:
ROASTED ANTIPASTI PLATTER

A delicious combination of Italian meats, cheeses and grilled veggies drizzled in a zesty Italian vinaigrette. It's the perfect grazing board to gather around and takes mere minutes to put together!

Add all of the herbed oil ingredients to a jar or a container and whisk to combine, then set aside.

Grill the fennel and asparagus. Drizzle 2–3 tablespoons of the herbed oil over the top and gently mix to coat them. In a ridged stovetop griddle pan set over a high temperature, add the vegetables and griddle for 2–5 minutes on each side until just slightly tender. Set aside.

To assemble the platter, cover most of the platter with salad leaves. Place the fresh mozzarella balls in a bowl and drizzle over 2–3 tablespoons of the herbed oil. Mix to combine, then place the bowl on the platter.

Next, add most of the grilled veggies, the tomatoes, Parmesan, assorted meats, artichoke hearts, stuffed peppers, the rest of the grilled veggies, the roasted peppers and the figs.

Finish it off by drizzling more of the herbed oil all over the platter and some balsamic glaze. Pour the remaining oil into a bowl for dipping.

Serve with crostini, breadsticks and crackers.

4 baby fennel

1 bunch of asparagus

200 g/7 oz. mixed salad leaves

200 g/7 oz. mini mozzarella balls

200 g/7 oz. cherry tomatoes on the vine

200 g/7 oz. Parmesan

150 g/5½ oz. prosciutto

100 g/3½ oz. assorted salamis, sliced

200 g/7 oz. marinated artichoke hearts

200 g/7 oz. sweet stuffed peppers

200 g/7 oz. roasted red (bell) peppers (home roasted or from a jar)

6 figs, halved

ITALIAN HERBED OIL

1 large chilli/chile, left whole

½ tsp crushed dried chilli/hot red pepper flakes

1 tsp black peppercorns, crushed

2 tsp dried oregano

2 tsp dried basil

2 garlic cloves, left whole

2 tsp sea salt

480 ml/2 cups olive oil

TO FINISH

100 ml/scant 1 cup balsamic glaze

crostini, breadsticks and crackers

SERVES 4

FARRO & COURGETTE SALAD

Farro is a wonderful whole grain with a nutty taste, which is packed full of nutrients. It works beautifully in this sharing salad.

Cook the farro in a saucepan of boiling salted water until al dente following the package instructions. Drain and spread on a tray to cool.

Meanwhile, briefly submerge the broad beans in a large saucepan of boiling salted water for 15 seconds, then plunge straight into a bowl of iced water (this makes them easier to peel). Drain, then slip the beans out of their skins. Combine the beans in a bowl with the cooked farro, courgettes, barberries, spring onions, marinated artichokes and herbs.

For the dressing, in a small bowl, stir together the garlic, olive oil, vinegar and sumac and season to taste. Pour onto the salad and toss to combine. Scatter with the pistachios to garnish.

250 g/1¼ cups farro

200 g/generous 1½ cups broad/fava beans, podded

2 courgettes/zucchini, spiralized

20 g/¾ oz. barberries, soaked in water and drained (or dried sour cherries)

4 spring onions/scallions, finely chopped

100 g/3½ oz. marinated artichokes, drained and quartered

handful fresh flat-leaf parsley, roughly chopped

small handful each fresh dill and chives, thinly sliced

sea salt and freshly ground black pepper

large handful of pistachios, to garnish

DRESSING

2 garlic cloves, crushed

100 ml/generous ⅓ cup extra virgin olive oil

50 ml/3½ tbsp red wine vinegar

½ tsp ground sumac

SERVES 4

FATTOUSH

A classic Middle Eastern salad, which makes a crunchy light side dish alongside other types of mezze or a great lunchbox filler – it's sprinkled with sumac, mint and parsley.

Heat the olive oil in a large saucepan over a medium heat, and, when hot, add half the bread and fry until golden. Drain on kitchen paper, then repeat with the remaining bread.

Combine the tomatoes, cucumber, parsley, mint, red pepper, radishes and spring onions in a large bowl and stir to combine.

Coarsely break the fried bread into smaller pieces and toss with the vegetable mixture. Sprinkle over the sumac, drizzle with extra virgin olive oil and lemon juice and mix gently to combine. Scatter over the pomegranate seeds, drizzle with pomegranate molasses and serve immediately.

100 ml/scant 1 cup olive oil

2 pieces of Middle Eastern bread, quartered

500 g/3 cups small cherry tomatoes, halved

2 small cucumbers, finely chopped

30 g/1 cup fresh flat-leaf parsley, coarsely chopped

30 g/1 cup fresh mint, leaves picked and coarsely chopped

1 red (bell) pepper, deseeded and finely chopped

100 g/3½ oz. radishes, thinly sliced

6 spring onions/scallions, thinly sliced

1 tbsp sumac

80 ml/⅓ cup extra virgin olive oil

2 tbsp fresh lemon juice

½ pomegranate, seeds only

1 tbsp pomegranate molasses

SERVES 4

PEA & PROSCUITTO SALAD

This salad is perfect alongside a pasta dish. It looks pretty, green and wild on the plate and the quince paste brushed onto the prosciutto really enhances the sweet and salty notes, which mixes really well with all the greens.

Preheat the oven to 200°C/180°C fan/400°F/Gas 6.

In a small bowl, mix the quince paste or honey with the mustard and olive oil and brush onto the prosciutto slices. Place the slices on a baking sheet lined with baking paper and bake for 8–10 minutes, checking that they don't overcook and get too brittle.

Meanwhile, blanch the sugarsnaps and mange tout until bright green, drain and refresh, and drain again.

Blanch the peas until bright green, drain and refresh, and drain again.

Combine the vegetables in a large bowl with the herbs, olive oil and sherry vinegar, season to taste and serve topped with the crispy prosciutto slices and pea shoots.

1 tbsp quince paste (or honey)

½ tsp Dijon mustard

1 tsp olive oil

170 g/6 oz. prosciutto slices (approx 2 packs)

500 g/1 lb. 2 oz. sugarsnap peas

500 g/1 lb. 2 oz. mange tout/ snow peas

200 g/1½ cups frozen peas, defrosted

2 tbsp fresh tarragon, coarsely torn

20 g/⅔ cup fresh mint, leaves picked

60 ml/¼ cup extra virgin olive oil

40 ml/2½ tbsp sherry vinegar

10 g/¼ cup pea shoots

SERVES 4

PIYAZ, TZATZIKI & SEEDED CRISPBREAD

A Turkish-style bean salad is paired here with a tangy pickled yogurt and cucumber dip and perfectly seedy crispbreads.

Preheat the oven to 180°C/160°C fan/350°F/Gas 4. For the crispbread, add the dried ingredients to a very large bowl, stir with your hands, then tip in the oil and water. Stir very well to mix together.

Take three sheets of parchment paper and place two baking sheets on them. Pull up on all sides of the paper to form the shape of the trays. This will be your rolling guide. Halve the dough and place on one piece of paper, then lay another piece of paper on top. Roll as thinly as you can, patching and shaping as you go. Peel off the top paper and lay the dough with the underneath paper on one of the baking sheets. Lightly score into pieces with a sharp knife, if you wish. Repeat with the remaining dough.

Bake for 15 minutes. Swap the baking sheets around and bake for a further 15 minutes. Do another swap and bake for 10–15 minutes until quite golden. Let cool and break into pieces. Store in an airtight container for up to 2 weeks.

For the pickled cucumber tzatziki, mix all the ingredients together, season well and set aside.

For the piyaz, combine the onion and sumac in a bowl and mix well, then add the tomatoes, beans, parsley, olive oil and lemon juice. Season well.

Serve together on a sharing platter or table with the crispbreads and other small plates to make a mezze to share.

SEEDED CRISPBREAD

50 g/½ cup rolled/old-fashioned oats

150 g/1 cup rye flour

50 g/6 tbsp each ground flaxseeds/linseeds, sesame seeds, sunflower seeds and pumpkin seeds

1 tsp fennel seeds cracked

1 tsp black sesame seeds

1 tsp cumin seeds

¼ tsp dried chilli/hot red pepper flakes

1 tsp sea salt flakes

80 ml/⅓ cup extra virgin olive oil

60 ml/¼ cup warm water

PICKLED CUCUMBER TZATZIKI

150 g/5½ oz. cucumber, grated

finely grated zest and freshly squeezed juice of ½ a lemon

500 g/2¼ cups Greek yogurt

2 tbsp olive oil

1 garlic clove, crushed

70 g/2½ oz. pickled gherkins, julienned, plus 2 tsp gherkin water

sea salt and freshly ground black pepper

PIYAZ

1 red onion, thinly sliced

1 tsp ground sumac

300 g/10½ oz. cherry tomatoes, deseeded and diced

400-g/14-oz. can cannellini beans, drained

10g/½ cup finely shredded flat-leaf parsley

60 ml/¼ cup olive oil

freshly squeezed juice of 1 lemon

SERVES 4

SALADE DE CHEVRE
WITH EDIBLE FLOWERS

**What says Paris more than Salade de chèvre? I just love this salad
and I like to add the radicchio as it adds a complexity and a slight
bitterness. This pairs well with the walnuts and the creaminess of
the goat's cheese. The addition of the edible flowers is for aesthetics
– also inspired by the beauty of Paris.**

Preheat the oven to 200°C/180°C fan/400°F/Gas 6.

Spread the walnuts over a baking sheet. Bake in the preheated
oven for 5 minutes or until lightly toasted. Set aside to cool.

Whisk the vinegar, oil, mustard and honey in a bowl and set aside.

Preheat the grill/broiler to medium-high. Cut the goat's cheese into
12 slices. Place the bread on a baking sheet and cook under the grill/
broiler for 1 minute on each side or until light and golden. Turn and top
each slice with a piece of goat's cheese. Spread the cheese to the edges
of the toast and top with the thyme. Cook under the grill/broiler for
2 minutes or until the cheese softens.

Meanwhile, tear the salad leaves into a bowl and mix well.
Lightly drizzle with half of the dressing and place onto
6 plates or a large platter. Top with goat's cheese toasts
and walnuts, then drizzle over the rest of the dressing
and top with edible flowers.

120 g/¾ cup walnut halves,
  toasted

2 tbsp sherry vinegar

60 ml/4 tbsp walnut oil

2 tsp Dijon mustard

a drizzle of honey

240 g/1¾ cups goat's cheese

1 sourdough baguette, cut
  diagonally into 12 slices

12 sprigs of fresh thyme

1 head butter lettuce

1 radicchio (pink, if in season)

1 small red gem lettuce

a punnet of edible flowers

SERVES 6

GRILLED WATERMELON & FETA SALAD

A beautifully refreshing summer salad that is ideal for serving at a barbecue party alongside grilled meat and vegetables and perfect for scaling up to feed large crowds.

Grease a ridged stovetop griddle pan with cooking oil spray and place over a high heat. Griddle the watermelon and the lemon half, flesh-side down, for about 2 minutes.

Carefully turn the watermelon on its side and cook for a further 2 minutes. Remove the lemon from the pan and set aside. Repeat the turning and cooking process on the other side of the watermelon so that all sides are charred.

Combine the herbs, rocket and tomatoes in a bowl. Drizzle with a little olive oil and toss to coat. Season with salt.

Place the grilled watermelon on a plate, top with the feta slices and the herb salad. Season with salt and pepper and serve the grilled lemon on the side for squeezing over.

cooking oil spray, for greasing

1 x 10-cm/4-inch x 4-cm/1½-inch chunk watermelon, skin and seeds removed

½ lemon

½ bunch fresh flat-leaf parsley leaves

½ bunch fresh mint leaves

30 g/1½ cups wild rocket/ arugula

300 g/10½ oz. mixed tomatoes, quartered

extra virgin olive oil, to drizzle

100 g/3½ oz. feta, cut into thick slices

sea salt and freshly ground black pepper

SERVES 4

WHEATBERRIES, CHORIZO, ORANGE, OLIVE & RADICCHIO SALAD

If you can get blood oranges, they look just stunning in this recipe, but if they are not in season you can use normal oranges. This is one of those dishes that looks beautiful when you bring it to the table and tastes just as good.

Peel and chop the oranges and place in a serving dish. Add the onion, olive oil, honey, dried chilli flakes, toasted cumin and coriander seeds and black olives. Stir together and set aside to marinate for at least 1 hour in the serving dish.

While all those flavours are melding, cook the wheatberries according to the package instructions, drain and add to the orange mixture while still warm – this will help all the flavours infuse more.

Heat a drizzle of oil in a large frying pan/skillet. Cook the chorizo slices for 4–5 minutes, until they are sizzling. Add to the serving dish with all the other ingredients, reserving the pan juices.

Finish with radicchio and parsley and serve drizzled with all the juices from the chorizo pan.

4 blood oranges

1 red onion, thinly sliced

2 tbsp olive oil, plus a drizzle for frying

2 tbsp runny honey

a pinch of dried chilli/hot red pepper flakes

1 tbsp cumin seeds, toasted

1 tbsp coriander seeds, toasted

100 g/1 cup stoned/pitted Kalamata olives

200 g/generous 1 cup wheatberries

1 chorizo ring, chopped into discs

2 heads radicchio

20 g/¾ oz. fresh flat-leaf parsley, leaves picked

SERVES 4

BEETROOT, BLOOD ORANGE & HORSERADISH SALAD

A beautiful salad to adorn any table, full of thirst-quenching orange, which pairs beautifully with the earthy beetroot/beet. The horseradish dressing also works well with any roast beef dish.

Preheat the oven to 200°C/180°C fan/400°F/Gas 6.

Place the beetroots in a roasting pan and fill with 1 cm/⅜ inch of hot water. Drizzle with 1½ tablespoons of the oil and season with salt and pepper. Cover the pan with foil and roast in the preheated oven for 45–50 minutes, turning occasionally, until tender. The cooking time will vary depending on the size of the vegetables. Peel and chop the beets into quarters and set aside.

Meanwhile, warm the remaining olive oil and the butter in a saucepan over a medium-high heat. Add the blood orange slices and cook for 1–2 minutes on each side until caramelized, then remove and set aside. Add the spinach to the pan, season with salt and pepper and allow to gently wilt.

Place the wilted spinach and blood oranges on a platter, then top with the roasted beetroot, chives and pumpkin seeds, if using.

To make the dressing, mix the creamed horseradish with the buttermilk and season with salt and pepper. Drizzle the dressing over the salad, sprinkle with thyme and serve with your favourite hummus, if liked.

1 bunch each purple and golden beetroot/beets, scrubbed, skins left on

2–3 candy beetroot/beet, scrubbed, skins left on

2½ tbsp olive oil

1 tbsp butter

3 blood oranges, peeled and sliced into rounds

200 g/7 oz. baby spinach

½ bunch fresh chives, halved

20 g/2 tbsp pumpkin seeds, toasted (optional)

sea salt and freshly ground black pepper

hummus, to serve (optional)

HORSERADISH DRESSING

2 tbsp creamed horseradish

50 ml/3½ tbsp buttermilk

pinch of fresh thyme, to garnish

SERVES 4

INSALATA PRIMAVERA WITH GRAINS, GOAT'S CHEESE & FRESH MINT DRESSING

Primavera means 'spring' in Italian and this dish is the epitome of spring. It is perfect to share, as a side to a pasta dish or to accompany a barbecue. The mixture of spring vegetables – asparagus, courgettes/zucchini and broad/fava beans – fresh goat's cheese and a minty dressing results in a salad that you will make time and time again.

For the mint dressing, mix the ingredients together in a bowl and season to taste.

Combine the quinoa, asparagus, courgette, broad beans, spring onions, parsley and chives in a large bowl. Drizzle with the mint dressing to taste and toss lightly to combine.

Scatter with soft salad leaves and goat's cheese, then drizzle with extra dressing and serve.

200 g/generous 1 cup quinoa, cooked according to package instructions

2 bunches asparagus, trimmed and thinly sliced lengthways on a mandoline

3 courgettes/zucchini, thinly sliced lengthways on a mandoline

300 g/1½ cups shelled broad/fava beans, peeled

1 bunch spring onions/ scallions, thinly sliced

a small handful of fresh parsley and a few chives, finely chopped

150 g/5½ oz. soft salad leaves

200 g/7 oz. soft goat's cheese, crumbled

FRESH MINT DRESSING

100 ml/scant ½ cup extra-virgin olive oil

30 g/1 oz. fresh mint, leaves picked and finely chopped

finely grated zest and juice of 1 lemon

1 tbsp apple cider vinegar

1 garlic clove, crushed

pinch of sugar

sea salt and freshly ground black pepper

SERVES 4

FREEKEH & HERB SALAD WITH PRESERVED LEMON & BLACK OLIVES

Roasted shallots with a touch of cinnamon serve as a bed for the freekeh, crisp cucumber, tomatoes, olives and the intense citrus but yet mellow preserved lemon. For an extra element, crumble over feta or add pan-fried halloumi.

Preheat the oven to 200°C/180°C fan/400°F/Gas 6.

Spread the shallots on a small baking sheet. Drizzle with the olive oil, sprinkle with cinnamon and oregano and season to taste. Roast in the preheated oven for 40–45 minutes until tender and caramelized.

Meanwhile, bring 400 ml/1¾ cups water and 1 teaspoon salt to the boil in a saucepan over a medium-high heat. Add the freekeh, stir, bring back to the boil and cover with a lid. Reduce the heat to low and cook for 25–30 minutes until the freekeh is tender and the water evaporates. Drain and transfer to a bowl.

Mix the dressing ingredients in a serving dish, then add the shallots, freekeh, cucumber and tomatoes and mix well. Check for seasoning, then add the herbs and scatter over the almonds. Serve with the addition of crumbled feta or pan-fried halloumi, if you wish.

8 shallots, peeled and halved

2 tbsp olive oil

a pinch of ground cinnamon

a pinch of dried oregano

200 g/7 oz. freekeh, rinsed

1 large cucumber, cubed

200 g/7 oz. cherry tomatoes, quartered

1 small bunch each fresh dill, coriander/cilantro, mint and parsley, leaves picked

50 g/generous ⅓ cup almonds, coarsely chopped and toasted

sea salt and freshly ground black pepper

feta or pan-fried halloumi, to serve (optional)

DRESSING

100 g/1 cup black olives, stoned/pitted and halved

1 preserved lemon, pith and flesh discarded, skin rinsed and finely chopped

1 garlic clove, crushed

60 ml/¼ cup olive oil

a pinch of ground cinnamon (optional)

freshly squeezed juice of 1–2 lemons, to taste

1 tsp honey, or to taste

SERVES 4

ROASTED VEG WITH PESTO & LEAFY SALAD

I could eat this every day with many variations of roasted vegetables, but my all-time favourite combo is roasted tomatoes with peppers. In my fridge there is always a batch of these tomatoes and they can really make a meal, whether it's breakfast, lunch, dinner or snack. On toast they are great with avocado, feta and rocket/arugula.

Preheat the oven to 200°C/180°C fan/400°F/Gas 6.

Place the tomatoes and peppers on a baking sheet lined with baking parchment. Drizzle with the olive oil, honey, dried chilli flakes and salt and pepper. Bake in the preheated oven for 20 minutes until just cooked through, then allow to cool.

Place the roasted vegetables and all their juices on a serving plate and top with the rocket and pesto.

270 g/1½ cups cherry tomatoes on the vine

200 g/1½ cups mixed yellow and red romano peppers, roughly chopped

2 tbsp olive oil

1 tsp honey

pinch of dried chilli/hot red pepper flakes

handful of rocket/arugula

1 tbsp pesto

sea salt and freshly ground black pepper

SERVES 6 AS A SIDE

ENERGIZING

SPICY ASIAN SALADS, PACKED WITH HEAT & SWEETNESS

SHARING PLATTER: COCONUT POACHED SHRIMP & FISH WITH ASIAN GREENS, GRAPEFRUIT DRESSING & STICKY CHILLI CASHEWS

This fresh and lively citrus salad makes a gorgeous appetizer, side salad or delicious lunch. You'll find it unique and refreshing, and so will your guests.

First, prepare the prawns. Place the coconut milk, fish sauce, soy sauce, galangal, lime leaves, shallots, chillies and lemongrass in a saucepan and bring to a simmer over a medium-high heat to infuse for about 8–10 minutes. Add the prawns and simmer for about 1–2 minutes until they just begin to colour, then remove from the heat. Stir in the lime juice and leave to stand to let the residual heat cook the prawns through for 1–2 minutes. Remove the cooked prawns and then return the pan to the heat to reduce the cooking liquor by half.

Combine all the dressing ingredients together in a cup, stirring well to dissolve the sugar.

For the sticky chilli cashews, preheat the oven to 200°C/180°C fan/400°F/Gas 6. Place the cashews on a baking sheet lined with baking paper. Drizzle with the oil, soy sauce, honey, sweet chilli sauce and brown sugar and mix well. Bake for 10 minutes, turning once or twice, until sticky.

On a platter, place the noodles, grapefruit, cucumber, carrots, spinach, toasted coconut and top with the prawns. Drizzle with the dressing, mix well and top with the sticky chilli cashews and the mixed fresh herbs. Serve some of the cooking liquor on the side.

800 ml/3½ cups coconut milk

1 tbsp fish sauce

1 tbsp soy sauce

20 g/¾ oz. galangal, thickly sliced

4 lime leaves, thinly sliced

2 shallots, thinly sliced

2 small red chillies/chiles, thinly sliced, plus extra (optional) to serve

1 lemongrass stalk, bruised

20 uncooked prawns/shrimp, peeled and cleaned

grated zest and juice of 2 limes, plus extra wedges to serve

300 g/11½ oz. fresh rice noodles, cooked

1 pink grapefruit, peeled and segmented

1 long cucumber, shaved lengthways

1 carrot, shaved lengthways

100 g/2 cups baby spinach

30 g/¾ cup toasted shaved coconut

100 g/3 cups mixed Thai or holy basil, mint and coriander/cilantro, leaves picked

DRESSING

juice of 1 pink grapefruit

juice of 1 lime

3 tbsp fish sauce

1 tbsp soy sauce

2–3 tbsp brown sugar (or to taste)

1–2 teaspoons Thai chilli sauce, to taste

STICKY CHILLI CASHEWS

80 g/⅔ cup raw cashews

1 tbsp flavourless oil

2 tbsp soy sauce

1 tbsp honey

1 tbsp sweet chilli sauce

1 tsp brown sugar

SERVES 2

CAULIFLOWER LARB
WITH COCONUT RICE
& FRESH LEAVES

Larb is a delicious dish from Northern Thailand that is usually made with meat and served as a salad with rice and crisp leaves. This is my fragrant, sweet and tangy cauliflower version.

Heat a wok or a large, heavy-based frying pan/skillet over a medium-high heat. Add the coconut chips and cook, stirring, for 2 minutes or until golden brown. Remove from the heat. Transfer to the bowl of a food processor and process until finely ground. Set aside.

Heat the oil in the wok or frying pan over a high heat. Add the cauliflower, lemongrass, lime leaves, chillies, soy sauce and lime juice and cook, stirring occasionally, for 5 minutes or until the cauliflower changes colour. Transfer to a bowl and set aside for 15 minutes to cool.

Toss the spring onions, coriander and mint into the cauliflower mixture. Season with salt. Serve with lettuce leaves and cooked jasmine rice mixed with the finely ground toasted coconut. Garnish with purple basil leaves, if you like.

30 g/¾ cup coconut chips

3 tbsp vegetable oil

1 large cauliflower, finely chopped

1 lemongrass stalk, tough outer layers removed, finely chopped

4 fresh lime leaves, thinly sliced

3 green Thai chillies/chiles, finely chopped

4 tbsp soy sauce

freshly squeezed juice of 1 lime

5 spring onions/scallions, thinly sliced

10 g/½ cup fresh coriander/ cilantro, leaves picked and chopped

10 g/½ cup fresh mint, leaves picked and chopped

sea salt

TO SERVE

lettuce leaves

cooked jasmine rice

purple basil (optional)

SERVES 4

ZINGY CRAB SALAD
& CRISPY TOASTS

**An elegant appetizer for a dinner party or perfect for date
night, full of fresh and zingy ingredients.**

For the dressing, place the vinegar, fish sauce, brown sugar and
2 tablespoons water in a small saucepan over a low heat, stirring
occasionally, for about 5 minutes until the sugar dissolves. Turn
off the heat and add the lime juice, garlic, chilli and coriander.
Transfer to a large bowl and leave to cool for 10 minutes.

For the crispy toasts, preheat the oven to 200°C/180°C fan/400°F/
Gas 6. Line a baking sheet with baking paper and place the flatbreads
on it. Brush the flatbreads with oil, sprinkle with salt and pepper and
bake for 10 minutes, turning once.

To the bowl containing the dressing, add the limes, shallots, half of
the crab, chives, lemongrass and peanuts. Season to taste and toss
to combine. Leave to marinate for 10 minutes before serving.

Place the leaves on a platter and top with the dressed crab, adding
the remaining reserved crab on top. Season with salt and pepper
and finish with lime zest, snipped chives and mayo on the side for
a creaminess. Place the flatbread shards on top and share.

2 limes, peeled and segmented
(reserve the zest to garnish

2 shallots, thinly sliced

300 g/11½ oz. crab meat

20 g/⅔ cup fresh chives, finely
chopped, plus extra to taste

1 lemongrass stalk, white part
only, thinly sliced

30 g/¼ cup roasted peanuts,
coarsely chopped

2 little gems, leaves separated

Japanese mayonnaise, to serve

ZINGY DRESSING

2 tbsp rice wine vinegar

2 tbsp fish sauce

2 tbsp brown sugar

60 ml/¼ cup fresh lime juice

2 garlic cloves, crushed

1 green chilli/chile, seeds
removed and finely chopped

1 tbsp freshly chopped
coriander/cilantro

CRISPY TOASTS

3 flatbreads, cut into shards

1 tbsp flavourless oil

sea salt and freshly ground
black pepper

SERVES 2

THAI PORK SALAD

A delightful Thai pork salad seasoned with a wonderful dressing made with lime, ginger, chilli and fish sauce. Super tasty, nice and light, but completely filling at the same time, which makes it an ideal summer meal.

For the marinade, combine the ingredients in a food processor and blend to a smooth paste.

Place the pork in a non-reactive container, pour the marinade over, turn to coat and leave to marinate for 10 minutes.

Heat a barbecue or ridged stovetop griddle pan to medium-high heat.

Drain the pork, then grill on the hot barbecue or griddle, turning occasionally, until cooked through. Leave to rest for 5 minutes, then thinly slice.

Meanwhile, toss the herbs, mango, cucumbers, baby gem, spring onions, shallots, lime leaves, lime juice and zest, fish sauce and chilli in a bowl to combine and adjust the seasoning to taste.

Add the pork and serve with steamed coconut rice if wanting to make a more substantial meal.

1 kg/2¼ lb. pork fillet, trimmed, split in half lengthways

100 g/3 cups fresh mint, coriander/cilantro and Thai basil

1 mango, thinly sliced

3 small cucumbers, sliced diagonally

2 baby gem lettuce, leaves separated

3 spring onions/scallions, thinly sliced

3 shallots, thinly sliced on a mandolin

3 lime leaves, thinly shredded

grated zest and juice of 2 limes

2 tbsp fish sauce

½ tsp chilli/chili powder

steamed coconut rice, to serve (optional)

MARINADE

1 large bunch fresh coriander/cilantro

3 garlic cloves, finely chopped

1 lemongrass stalk (white part only), finely chopped

2 tbsp palm sugar/ jaggery

1 tbsp fish sauce

1 tbsp dark soy sauce

SERVES 4

SAMBAL SMASHED CUCUMBER WITH TOFU & BROCCOLI

Sambal smashed cucumber, crispy tofu and broccoli is the perfect salad combination. It can be a side for a selection of other Asian dishes to feed a larger crowd, but also perfect with steamed rice for a clean and healthy meal.

Rinse the cucumbers and wrap in clingfilm/plastic wrap. Use a rolling pin to gently smash the cucumber (not so if falls apart), just until it flattens a bit and splits. Remove the plastic and cut into four long lengths, then into bite-sized pieces. Pop the cucumber into a sieve/strainer and toss in the sugar and salt. Leave for 30 minutes to drain.

To make a marinade, place the garlic, yuzu, vinegar, soy sauce, chilli flakes, Sichuan pepper and sesame oil in a wide mixing bowl and stir well.

Meanwhile, in a saucepan of boiling water, blanch and refresh the broccoli so it's firm and still bright green.

In a frying pan/skillet over a medium–high heat, add the flavourless oil and cook the tofu for 4–6 minutes on each side until crispy. Transfer to kitchen paper until ready to use.

Shake the cucumber of any excess liquid and add to the bowl with the marinade. Toss in the broccoli and tofu. Turn it all over with your hands or a thin bowled-spoon and tip onto a serving dish. Shower with the toasted sesame seeds to finish.

2 cucumbers (a long, thin variety if possible)

2 tsp caster/granulated sugar

2 tsp sea salt

2 garlic cloves, crushed

1 tbsp yuzu juice

1 tbsp rice vinegar

1 tbsp soy sauce

½ tsp dried chilli/hot red pepper flakes (Korean if possible)

1 tsp Sichuan peppercorns, toasted and crushed

1 tsp sesame oil

200 g/7 oz. tenderstem broccoli

2 tbsp flavourless oil

250 g/9 oz. tofu, patted dry and cubed

1 tbsp Chinese chilli/chili oil

2 tbsp sesame seeds, toasted

SERVES 2

SAUERKRAUT

A classic fermented salad dish that makes a great addition to any meal. Keep a jar in the fridge to pep up lunches and dinners.

Put the cabbage, salt and caraway seeds in a bowl and toss to combine, then massage the salt and spices into the cabbage briefly. Leave to stand for about 30 minutes until the cabbage starts to wilt. Transfer to the jar and press to pack the cabbage down.

Pour in water to just cover the cabbage and top with a small plastic sandwich bag filled with water to keep the cabbage submerged. Put the lid on the jar and set aside at room temperature for 1–2 days until bubbles appear on top. Refrigerate, covered with clingfilm/plastic wrap with a hole pierced in the top for 3 days before using.

The sauerkraut will keep in the fridge for about 1 month; the flavour will get stronger as it ages.

450 g/1 lb. Savoy or white cabbage (about ½), core removed and thinly sliced

1 tbsp sea salt

1 tsp caraway seeds

1 x sterilized litre/quart jar

MAKES 1 JAR

COURGETTE, CARROT & HORSERADISH SALAD WITH WATERCRESS

A light, punchy side salad to accompany any meat dish.

Mix the courgettes and carrots in a serving dish and dress with the lemon juice, olive oil and some salt and pepper. Leave to sit for about 30 minutes, then top with the watercress. Toss after you take to the table, then grate horseradish over the top to finish.

200 g/1½ cups mini courgettes/zucchini, thinly sliced lengthways

200 g/7 oz. chantenay carrots, thinly sliced lengthways

juice of ½ lemon

3 tbsp olive oil

100 g/1 cup watercress

½ tsp fresh horseradish, grated or 1 tsp cream horseradish

sea salt and freshly ground black pepper

SERVES 6 AS A SIDE

MISO BROWN RICE SALAD WITH TOFU & GINGER DRESSING

This is a salad packed with nourishing elements that I could eat every day for lunch or dinner. It is definitely one of those dishes that you can make on a Sunday for your prep-ahead lunches. It travels well, and the miso ginger dressing is all it needs for a toasty, savoury and fresh finish.

First, make the dressing. Mix all the ingredients together and set aside.

Preheat the oven to 220°C/200°C fan/425°F/Gas 7.

Wrap the tofu in paper towels or a kitchen towel and place on a baking sheet. Weigh down with something heavy, like a frying pan/skillet and let it sit for 10 minutes. Unpack and unwrap tofu, then transfer to a cutting board and cut into 5-cm/2-inch cubes.

Whisk together the ginger, soy sauce, white miso, honey and chilli flakes. Add the tofu and gently toss to coat. Sprinkle cornflour over it all and mix until incorporated. Leave to sit for 10 minutes.

Remove the tofu from the marinade and spread the cubes out on a baking sheet lined with baking paper. Bake in the preheated oven for 25–30 minutes, turning halfway through, until golden brown and a thin crust forms.

Divide the rice between 2 plates, then top with edamame, sliced radishes, beetroot and roasted tofu. Drizzle with the dressing and finish with coriander and dried chilli flakes.

250 g/generous 1¼ cups brown sushi rice, cooked according to package instructions

200 g/7 oz. edamame beans

100 g/3½ oz. radishes, sliced

2 golden beetroot/beets, grated

handful of fresh coriander/cilantro

pinch of dried chilli/hot red pepper flakes

GINGER DRESSING

thumb-sized piece of fresh ginger, grated

4 spring onions/scallions, thinly sliced

3 tbsp white miso

1 garlic clove, crushed

1 tbsp rice vinegar

2 tbsp sesame oil

TOFU

300-g/10½-oz. pack tofu

thumb-sized piece of fresh ginger, grated

60 ml/¼ cup soy sauce

2 tbsp white miso

2 tbsp honey

pinch of dried chilli/hot red pepper flakes

1 tbsp cornflour/cornstarch

SERVES 2

WILD RICE, CAULIFLOWER & GOLDEN RAISIN SALAD

This is my favourite salad ever. Everything comes together in perfect harmony – sweet, tang, nutty, savoury and crunch.

Heat half the olive oil in a saucepan over a medium-high heat. Add the onion and garlic and fry for about 4–5 minutes until tender.

Add the rice, stir to coat, then add the stock. Season to taste and bring to the boil. Cover with a lid, then reduce the heat to low and cook for 30–40 minutes until the rice is tender and the stock is absorbed. Remove from the heat and leave to stand, covered, to steam for about 15 minutes.

Meanwhile, preheat the oven to 220°C/200°C fan/425°F/Gas 7.

Toss the cauliflower with the remaining oil in a bowl and season to taste with salt and pepper. Spread out on the lined baking sheet and roast in the preheated oven, stirring occasionally, for about 15 minutes until tender and golden.

Cook the butter in a saucepan over a high heat, swirling the pan occasionally, for about 4–5 minutes until nut brown. Remove from the heat and stir in the hazelnuts, sultanas, vinegar and lemon zest and juice.

Serve the pilaf warm, topped with the cauliflower, drizzled with the burnt butter and sprinkled with the parsley and mint.

2 tbsp olive oil

1 red onion, thinly sliced

1 garlic clove, finely crushed

175 g/6 oz. wild rice

500–750 ml/2–3 cups vegetable stock (depending on the rice)

300 g/10½ oz. tenderstem cauliflower

40 g/3 tbsp butter

30 g/¼ cup hazelnuts, roasted and coarsely chopped

30 g/scant ¼ cup sultanas/ golden raisins, coarsely chopped

1 tbsp sherry vinegar

grated zest and freshly squeezed juice of ½ lemon

sea salt and freshly ground black pepper

freshly chopped flat-leaf parsley and mint, to serve

SERVES 4

TAMARIND RICE SALAD WITH CRAB & GREEN CHILLIES

Tamarind, with its sour-sweet tang akin to apricots and lemons, really brings this rice and green chilli/chile salad to life. The dish is full of different textures and the carmargue rice, cooling cucumber, puffed spelt, luxurious crab meat and spicy green chillies make this salad perfect for entertaining, be it a summer barbecue, a light lunch or sharing with friends.

In a serving bowl, place the rice, cucumber and red onion and set aside.

Make the tamarind dressing, by mixing all the ingredients together, taste for seasoning and add 3 tablespoons water to loosen. Add to the rice mixture and set aside to infuse.

Meanwhile, preheat the oven to 200°C/180°C fan/400°F/Gas 6.

Place the puffed spelt and peanuts on a baking sheet and toast in the preheated oven until golden. Leave to cool.

Add the crab to the rice mixture, then top with the toasted puffed spelt and peanuts. To finish, add the herbs, green chilli and spring onions and lime wedges for squeezing.

200 g/generous 1 cup red carmargue rice, cooked according to package instructions and cooled

1 long cucumber, halved, seeds removed and cut in half moons

½ red onion, thinly sliced

20 g/scant 1 cup puffed spelt

40 g/⅓ cup peanuts, coarsely crushed

400 g/14 oz. white crab meat

a handful each fresh mint and coriander/cilantro, leaves picked

1 long green chilli/chile, thinly sliced diagonally

4 spring onions/scallions, thinly sliced

lime wedges, to serve

TAMARIND DRESSING

1 tbsp tamarind paste

20 g/1 cup each fresh mint and coriander/cilantro

1 long green chilli/chile, finely chopped

1 garlic clove, crushed

1 tsp ground cumin

freshly squeezed juice of 2 limes

1 tsp honey or to taste

3 tbsp olive oil

2 tbsp good-quality mayonnaise

SERVES 4

KAREDOK SALAD

A salty and crunchy salad, perfect for pairing with pan-fried salmon or other fish.

Gently toss all the ingredients for the salad together and arrange on a serving platter.

In a food processor, pulse together all the ingredients for the dressing until coarsely blitzed, and serve drizzled over the salad.

200 g/7 oz. fine green/
French beans, cooked
and cut into 3-cm/
1-inch lengths

1 small Chinese cabbage,
thinly sliced (on a
mandoline preferably)

1 large cucumber,
cut into julienne

100 g/1¾ cups
beansprouts

a handful fresh Thai basil

4 shallots, thinly sliced
into rounds

DRESSING

2–3 tbsp peanut/
groundnut oil

150 g/1¼ cups unsalted
peanuts, toasted

1 tsp galangal paste

1–2 red chillies/chiles,
chopped

2 garlic cloves, roughly
chopped

freshly squeezed juice
of 2–3 limes

2 tbsp palm sugar/
jaggery

2 tbsp light soy sauce

½ tsp shrimp paste

SERVES 4

WAKAME, PEAR & DAIKON SALAD

This is a salad of contrasts – sweet and peppery and minerally saltiness. It's surprisingly refreshing.

Place the wakame in a large bowl, cover with warm water and set aside to soak for 5 minutes, then drain well. If the wakame is in big pieces, chop it up into bitesize pieces (a similar size to the radish slices). Combine the radish and pears in a large bowl and add the drained wakame.

For the miso dressing, combine the soy sauce, rice wine, cider vinegar and lime juice in a bowl with 2 tablespoons water. Add the miso and whisk to combine.

Arrange the salad in a large serving bowl or on a plate, drizzle with the miso dressing and serve.

10 g/⅓ oz. dried wakame seaweed

50 g/2 oz. daikon, scrubbed and sliced on a mandoline

50 g/2 oz. radish, thinly sliced on a mandoline

2 pears (such as Williams), shaved on a mandoline

MISO DRESSING

1 tbsp light soy sauce

1 tbsp rice wine (mirin)

1 tablespoon cider vinegar

juice of 1 lime

2 tbsp shiro miso

SERVES 6

CRISPY SALMON, CLEMENTINE & NOODLE SALAD

This is a very easy midweek salad to serve the family but also can be elevated for a dinner party around the holiday season.

Coat the salmon fillet in the sweet chilli sauce. Heat the oil in a frying pan/skillet over a medium-high heat. Sear the salmon for 2–3 minutes on each side, leaving it a little pink in the middle. Place the salmon on a plate, cover loosely with foil and leave to rest for while you make the salad.

Prepare the noodles according to the package instructions, then drain and set aside.

Meanwhile, whisk all the dressing ingredients together in a large bowl until the sugar dissolves.

Add the cherry tomatoes, avocado and sliced red chilli to the dressing bowl and toss gently to combine. Add the noodles and herbs and gently toss to combine again.

Stir through the soy sauce and honey and finish by adding the mixed green vegetables, clementines and cashews.

500 g/1 lb. 2oz. skinless salmon fillet, pin-boned

1 tbsp sweet chilli sauce

1 tbsp sunflower oil

200 g/7 oz. egg noodles

200 g/1 cup cherry tomatoes, quartered

1 avocado, peeled, stoned/pitted and roughly chopped

1 small red chilli/chile, deseeded and thinly sliced

30 g/1 cup mixed fresh mint, coriander/cilantro and Thai or regular basil leaves

1 tbsp soy sauce

1 tbsp honey

200 g/7 oz. mixed green beans, sugarsnap peas and mange tout

2 clementines, peeled and segmented

2 tbsp salted cashews, roughly chopped

DRESSING

grated zest and juice of 1 lime juice

zest and juice of 2 clementines

2 tbsp fish sauce

2 tbsp sweet chilli sauce

1 tbsp flavourless oil

SERVES 4

NOURISHING

SUPERFOOD INGREDIENTS WITH ADDED NUTS, SEEDS & BEANS

SHARING PLATTER:
MEZZE SALAD SHARING PLATTER INCLUDING KISIR IN LETTUCE CUPS

This colourful mezze platter is loaded up with Middle Eastern dips, fresh veggies, olives and pita or flatbreads for the ultimate, graze-able snack board.

Whisk all of the dressing ingredients together in a bowl and season with salt and black pepper.

Cook the bulgur wheat according to the package directions. Leave to cool until just warm. Transfer to a medium bowl and mix in the dressing.

Meanwhile, toast the walnuts in a small frying pan/skillet over a medium heat, tossing often, for about 4 minutes until golden brown. Transfer to a cutting board, leave to cool slightly, then finely chop.

Add the walnuts, tomatoes, cucumber, spring onions, parsley, mint and pomegranate seeds to the bulgur, toss well and season to taste.

Arrange the lettuce leaves in a single layer on a platter and spoon some of the bulgur mixture into each leaf.

Add the labne in separate rounds around the lettuce leaves. I also like to place the feta now as it is another large item. Slice up your veggies and arrange them around the dips.

Place the pita bread or crackers into the remaining empty spots. Last fit the olives into any remaining spots. If desired, top with fresh herbs to add some extra flavour. Devour!

Note *If you don't finish your mezze board, you can wrap it in cling film/plastic wrap and place in the fridge for up to 5 days.*

DRESSING

5 tbsp extra-virgin olive oil

3 tbsp fresh lemon juice

3 tbsp pomegranate molasses

1 tbsp tomato purée/paste

1 tsp Aleppo dried chilli flakes

sea salt and freshly ground black pepper

FILLING

200 g/7 oz. bulgur wheat

50 g/⅓ cup walnuts

3 tomatoes, seeds removed and finely chopped

1 cucumber, finely chopped

3 spring onions/scallions, finely chopped

30 g/1 cup fresh parsley leaves, finely chopped, plus extra to garnish

30 g/1 cup fresh mint leaves, finely chopped, plus extra to garnish

100 g/½ cup pomegranate seeds

2 heads Little Gem lettuce, leaves separated

FOR THE PLATTER

100 g/3½ oz. labne

200 g/7 oz. feta cheese, cubed

6–8 mini cucumbers, sliced into sticks

10 small radishes, quartered

150 g/5½ oz. plum tomatoes

4–6 pita bread rounds

200 g/2 cups stoned/pitted green olives

SERVES 4–6

CAMARGUE RICE SALAD WITH PAN-FRIED APRICOTS & HALLOUMI

Apricots and halloumi pair beautifully in this dish of tangy sweet with salty cheese and earthy red Camargue rice. Camargue rice is grown in the eponymous region of south-eastern France, and it features a beautiful red russet colour and wonderful nutty taste.

Cook the rice according to the package instructions, leave to cool, then place on a serving platter.

Heat a non-stick frying pan/skillet over a medium heat. Add the halloumi and cook for 5–7 minutes, turning halfway, until the halloumi is golden. Remove from the pan. Add 1 tablespoon of the olive oil and pan-fry the apricots for 2–3 minutes until they soften, then turn them over and add the brown sugar and red wine vinegar. Return the halloumi to the pan.

Stir the spinach leaves into the rice, then add the celery and spoon the halloumi and apricot mixture, with all the juices, onto the rice on the platter. Finish with the pine nuts.

Make the dressing by mixing all the ingredients together in a small bowl or jar and serve alongside the rice and halloumi.

250 g/1⅓ cups Camargue rice

250 g/9 oz. halloumi, cut into strips

4 tbsp olive oil

3–4 apricots, stoned/pitted and chopped

1 tbsp brown sugar

1 tbsp red wine vinegar

100 g/3½ oz. baby spinach

2 celery stalks/ribs, thinly sliced

50 g/1¾ oz. toasted pine nuts

DRESSING

1 tsp Dijon mustard

1 tsp honey

30 ml/2 tbsp red wine vinegar

60 ml/¼ cup olive oil

1 teaspoon dried chilli/hot red pepper flakes (optional)

SERVES 4

SMOKED MACKEREL WITH ROASTED BEETROOT, WATERCRESS & WASABI DRESSING

This is one of those salads that can be plated in advance and dressed before serving. It can be served as an appetizer and individually plated or on a sharing plater. It pairs beautifully with a glass of fizz during the holiday season.

4 beetroot/beets, quartered (or 200 g/ 7 oz. baby beetroot/ beet with stalks)

6 tbsp olive oil

1 small celeriac, peeled and cut into fine matchsticks

juice of 1 lemon

2 tbsp cider vinegar

2 tbsp clear honey

2 tsp wasabi (or to taste)

100 g/2 cups watercress, washed and drained, larger stalks removed

small handful of fresh herbs, chopped (parsley, tarragon, chives)

4 smoked mackerel fillets, shredded (bones removed)

SERVES 4

Preheat the oven to 200°C/180°C fan/400°F/ Gas 6. Place the beetroot on a baking sheet with 2 tablespoons of the olive oil and season well. Bake in the oven for 40 minutes or until cooked through.

Meanwhile, toss the celeriac in a large bowl with the lemon juice.

In a small bowl, mix the vinegar, honey, wasabi and the remaining olive oil. Toss into the celeriac with the watercress, herbs and smoked mackerel. Add the beetroot and check the seasoning before serving.

ROASTED PUMPKIN, WINTER LEAVES, PINK PEPPERCORN LABNE & MINT & PISTACHIO DRESSING

For an easy and impressive dinner you can serve this directly from the roasting pan. This ensures that you don't waste a single drop of cooking juices. It looks just as beautiful arranged on a platter.

The day before, start by making the labne. Line a fine-mesh strainer with cheesecloth and set the strainer over a medium bowl. Spoon yogurt onto the muslin, wrap any overhanging muslin up and over the yogurt to cover and refrigerate overnight.

The next day, preheat the oven to 200°C/180°C fan/400°F/Gas 6.

Arrange the pumpkin in a large, shallow baking dish. Drizzle with olive oil and season with salt and pepper. Roast for 25–30 minutes, or until tender and lightly charred. Add the grapes, split into smaller bunches, for the final 5 minutes of roasting so they still hold their shape.

Meanwhile, place peppercorns, coriander seeds and fennel seeds in a small pan. Cook over a medium heat, stirring occasionally, for 2 minutes until fragrant. Gently crush in a pestle and mortar and set aside.

For the dressing, heat a small pan over a medium heat. Add the garlic cloves and cook for 7–10 minutes, or until the skins are browned and the cloves are softened. Remove and leave to cool.

Squeeze the garlic from their skins and place in a blender with half the herbs and the pistachios. Blend to mix and then gently pour in the oil. Remove from the blender and add the lemon juice and zest and the remaining chopped herbs.

On a serving platter, place the labne with the spice mix, top with the roasted pumpkin, drizzle with the dressing and finish with winter leaves.

1 kg/2¼ lb. pumpkin, cut into wedges

3 tbsp olive oil

1 bunch of red grapes

sea salt and freshly ground black pepper

50 g/1 cup mixed winter leaves, to finish

PINK PEPPERCORN LABNE

500 g/2 cups Greek yogurt

1½ tsp pink peppercorns

1 tsp coriander seeds

1 tsp fennel seeds

1 tsp sea salt

olive oil

DRESSING

4 large garlic cloves, unpeeled

20 g/⅔ cup fresh basil leaves

20 g/⅔ cup fresh mint leaves

100 g/¾ cup pistachios, shelled

80 ml/⅓ cup olive oil

grated zest and juice of 1 lemon

muslin/cheesecloth

SERVES 4

WHOLEGRAIN SALAD WITH EGGS & SHALLOT YOGURT DRESSING

Wholesome and satisfying, perfect substantial lunch or dinner salad that will keep you nourished.

Preheat the oven to 200°C/180°C fan/400°F/Gas 6.

Place the tomatoes on a baking sheet lined with baking paper, drizzle with olive oil and season well. Roast for 25–30 minutes or until the tomatoes are soft but still hold shape. Reserve the cooking juices for extra drizzling at the end.

Meanwhile, mix the shallot, yogurt, mint and 1 tablespoon of the lemon juice and zest in a small bowl. Season with salt and pepper.

Toss the greens with the cooked grains and the remaining lemon juice and zest in a medium bowl. Season with salt and pepper.

Spoon the shallot yogurt onto plates and top with a mess of salad, roasted tomatoes and the boiled or fried eggs. Drizzle with the reserved tomato cooking juices.

4 plum tomatoes, halved

2 tbsp olive oil

2 shallots, finely chopped

200 g/7 oz. Greek yogurt

20 g/⅔ cup fresh mint, leaves picked

grated zest and juice of ½ lemon

200 g/7 oz. mixed greens (rocket/arugula, mustard greens and spinach)

200 g/7 oz. mixed cooked whole grains (such as freekeh, wheatberries, millet)

4 eggs (either boiled or fried)

sea salt and freshly ground black pepper

SERVES 4

GREEN GODDESS CAULIFLOWER SALAD WITH TEMPEH

This is one of those good-for-your-body-and-soul salads. Personally, I prefer to quickly blanch the veg, still leaving a lot of bite, but you can also combine the ingredients raw if you prefer.

In a blender or high-speed food processor, blend all of the avocado mint dressing ingredients until smooth and creamy. Season to taste.

In a large bowl, take 60 ml/¼ cup of the dressing and massage it into the kale.

Divide the kale between 2 bowls and top with the cauliflower florets, Romanesco broccoli florets, sunflower seeds and pear slices – dividing each ingredient evenly between the bowls.

Heat the olive oil in a large frying pan/skillet over a medium-high heat and add the tempeh slices. Cook the tempeh on each side for a few minutes until golden brown and slightly caramelized.

Add the tempeh to each salad and top with more avocado mint dressing.

200 g/7 oz. kale, destemmed, chopped, blanched and refreshed

200 g/7 oz. cauliflower, cut into florets, blanched and refreshed

150 g/5½ oz. Romanesco broccoli, cut into florets, blanched and refreshed

60 g/scant ½ cup sunflower seeds, roasted

1 pear, cored and sliced

1 tbsp olive oil

200 g/7 oz. tempeh, sliced into 8 thin strips

edible flowers, to garnish (optional)

CREAMY AVOCADO MINT DRESSING

150 g/5½ oz. silken tofu

1 ripe avocado, peeled and pitted

large handful of fresh mint, leaves picked

freshly squeezed juice of ½ lemon

½ tbsp maple syrup

1 tsp apple cider vinegar

1 garlic clove, crushed

¼ tsp ground ginger

sea salt and freshly ground black pepper

SERVES 2 GENEROUSLY

AVOCADO & KALE GRAIN BOWL WITH TAHINI-CORIANDER DRESSING

These bowls can be prepared ahead for either a light lunch at home or for work meals for the week. Pouches of ready-cooked mixed grains, with extra seasonings added, can be bought from most supermarkets.

Combine the kale, olive oil and lemon juice and zest in a bowl, season and massage the kale with your fingers until it wilts. Add the spring onions, chickpeas and mixed grains and toss to combine.

For the dressing, whisk the ingredients together in a bowl, then thin with 2–3 tablespoons hot water to drizzling consistency and season to taste.

Divide the kale mixture between 2 serving bowls and scatter with the feta. Dip one half of the cut-side of the avocado in dukkah, place on top of the kale mixture and arrange the courgette and olives next to it. Drizzle with the dressing to taste and serve scattered with pistachio nuts.

1 bunch kale, stems discarded, torn into bite-sized pieces

3 tbsp extra virgin olive oil

finely grated zest and freshly squeezed juice of 2 lemons

4 spring onions/scallions, finely chopped

400-g/14-oz. can chickpeas/garbanzo beans, drained

400 g/14 oz. mixed cooked grains

120 g/4 oz. feta, crumbled (or vegan equivalent)

1 avocado, halved, stoned/pitted and peeled

2 tbsp dukkah, plus extra to finish

1 courgette/zucchini, grated

50 g/½ cup stoned/ pitted green olives

pistachio nuts, coarsely chopped, to serve

TAHINI-CORIANDER/ CILANTRO DRESSING

30 g/1 oz. fresh coriander/cilantro, leaves and stalks

1 tsp ground coriander

1 tsp ground cumin

70 ml/scant ⅓ cup extra virgin olive oil

60 ml/¼ cup tahini

1 garlic clove, crushed

freshly squeezed juice of 1 lemon

sea salt and freshly ground black pepper

SERVES 2

ANY TIME OF DAY MIDDLE EASTERN SALAD BOWL WITH BAHARAT DRESSING

This type of dish or variations of it will be eaten all over the Middle East and even at breakfast time. I think it can be eaten at any time of day as a main plate or a side.

Cook the eggs in a saucepan of boiling water (6 minutes for soft-boiled), then drain, cool under cold running water and peel.

For the baharat dressing, whisk the ingredients in a large bowl to combine.

Add the lentils, tomatoes, onion, radishes and herbs to the dressing, season to taste and toss to combine.

Serve warm topped with feta, the halved eggs and dill sprigs and sprinkled with sumac.

4 eggs, at room temperature
1 x 400 g/14 oz. can green or brown lentils, drained
400 g/2 cups mixed cherry tomatoes, halved
1 red onion, thinly sliced
8 radishes, sliced
30 g/1 cup fresh flat-leaf parsley, plus extra to serve
100 g/3½ oz. feta
2 tbsp coarsely chopped fresh dill, plus extra sprigs to serve
1 tsp sumac
sea salt and freshly ground black pepper

BAHARAT DRESSING
125 ml/½ cup extra-virgin olive oil
2 tbsp aged red wine vinegar
grated juice and zest of 1 lemon
1 tsp runny honey
1 garlic clove, crushed
1 tsp barahat

SERVES 4

BARLEY & WILD RICE WITH CANDIED SALTED ALMONDS & BARBERRIES

Candied salted almonds, tart and sour barberries, grains, sumac and dried rose petals – all evoke images of eastern feasts, mint tea, incense burning and people coming together. This rice dish can be served alongside slow roasts, barbecued meats and vegetables or on its own with crumbled soft goat's cheese.

For the candied salted almonds, preheat the oven to 200°C/180°C fan/ 400°F/Gas 6 and line a baking sheet with baking paper. Stir the sugar with 2 tablespoons water in a saucepan over a low heat until the sugar dissolves. Add the almonds, stir to coat, then tip onto the baking sheet and bake in the preheated oven for about 10 minutes, stirring occasionally, until lightly caramelized. Set aside.

Meanwhile, place the barley in a saucepan of cold salted water. Then place 200 g/generous 1 cup of the wild rice in a second pan of cold salted water. Bring both pans to the boil over a medium-high heat, then reduce to medium and simmer for 20–25 minutes, until tender but not falling apart. Drain and set aside.

To make the dressing, mix the olive oil, lemon juice, sumac, salt and sliced onion in a bowl and leave it to sit for at least 20 minutes.

Heat the vegetable oil in a saucepan to 200°C/400°F. Add the remaining wild rice and fry until puffed. Remove with a metal sieve/ strainer and drain on paper towels.

Toss the barley and wild rice with the barberries and the dressing, then tip into a serving bowl and scatter with rose petals, mint leaves, candied almonds and puffed wild rice. Crumble over the goat's cheese, if using, and serve.

150 g/generous ¾ cup barley

250 g/1⅓ cups wild rice

2 tbsp dried barberries

sea salt

vegetable oil, for deep-frying

CANDIED SALTED ALMONDS

2 tbsp light soft brown sugar

100 g/¾ cup salted Marcona almonds

DRESSING

60 ml/¼ cup olive oil

freshly squeezed juice of 2 lemons

2 tbsp sumac

1 tsp salt

1 red onion, thinly sliced

TO SERVE

2 tbsp dried rose petals

30 g/1 oz. fresh mint, leaves picked

soft goat's cheese, crumbled (optional)

SERVES 4 AS A SIDE

MIXED BRASSICA SALAD WITH HORSERADISH & LEMON DRESSING

Pure freshness on a plate with a fiery kick from the horseradish. The most important thing to remember here is to dress this simple salad well in advance of serving to give the vegetables time to soften slightly.

Blanch the peas in boiling water for 1–2 minutes or until bright green, then drain, refresh, drain again and set aside until needed.

For the dressing, whisk all the ingredients together in a bowl, season to taste and set aside.

Combine the cauliflower, cabbage, Brussels sprouts, radishes, herbs, chilli and half the Parmesan or vegetarian alternative, if using, in a large bowl and toss to combine. Add the lemon dressing, season to taste and mix until the cabbage begins to wilt.

Serve the salad scattered with the peas, the remaining cheese, if using, and extra herbs.

100 g/⅔ cup fresh peas

1 cauliflower, thinly sliced

200 g/7 oz. cabbage, shredded

200 g/7 oz. Brussels sprouts, shredded

150 g/5½ oz. small radishes, thinly sliced lengthways

20 g/1 cup each (loosely packed) fresh mint and flat-leaf parsley, torn, plus extra to garnish

1 long green chilli/chile, deseeded and finely chopped

80 g/1½ cups finely grated Parmesan (optional) or vegetarian alternative

sea salt and freshly ground black pepper

HORSERADISH LEMON DRESSING

fresh horseradish, grated, to taste

100 ml/⅓ cup extra-virgin olive oil

50 ml/3½ tbsp freshly squeezed lemon juice

SERVES 4-6

NURTURING

COMFORTING, SUBSTANTIAL SALADS WITH ADDED PROTEIN

SHARING PLATTER:
JAMON, PEACHES, ENDIVE, BLUE CHEESE & OLIVE PLATTER

A rustic platter full of delicious ingredients – the griddled peaches pair perfectly with the rich blue cheese to create a nourishing sharing platter for all.

Place the peaches in a medium bowl with a sprinkle of flaky salt and a drizzle of olive oil. Fold in gently with your hands and set aside. You want to keep the peach skin in tact.

Heat a ridged stovetop griddle pan to a medium–high heat and griddle the peaches for 1–2 minutes on each side just to colour them slightly. Set aside.

Heat the quince paste or honey in a small saucepan over a low heat for about 1 minute until loosened. Add the black pepper and swirl the pan around for 15 seconds. Remove from the heat, add the vinegar and swirl to combine.

In a shallow, rimmed serving bowl or platter, arrange the radicchio in sections along with the peaches, then add the jamon, weaving it among the peaches. Lastly, tuck in the blue cheese and olives here and there.

Spoon over the quince vinaigrette and sprinkle with the thyme and a little flaky salt. Serve with the baguette shards and enjoy with a chilled glass of white wine, Cava or whatever you like.

4 peaches, cut into large wedges or quarters

3 tbsp quince paste (or honey)

2 tsp coarsely ground black pepper

1 tbsp sherry vinegar

2 heads radicchio

8–10 slices Ibérican jamon

100 g/3½ oz. Danish blue cheese, crumbled

50 g/½ cup stoned/pitted green olives

flaky sea salt

TO FINISH

2–3 sprigs fresh thyme

baguette in long shards

SERVES 4

FETA & GRIDDLED WATERMELON PLATE WITH PINK PEPPERCORN & ALEPPO CHILLI-INFUSED OLIVE OIL & GREEN OLIVES

In this salad the feta has been softened to make it creamy and the watermelon has been griddled to give a charred taste and to caramelize the sugars, truly transforming simple ingredients into something far more exciting.

At least 1 hour before serving, infuse the olive oil by placing all the ingredients in a saucepan and gently bring to heat. Take care not to boil or burn the oil. Leave to cool and store in a clean glass jar or bottle until needed.

For the salad, brush a ridged stovetop griddle pan with oil and set over a medium heat. Add the watermelon to the pan and cook for about 2–3 minutes each side until charred on both sides. The idea is to create a charred flavour and caramelize the sugars in the fruit, not to cook it, so it is best to have the griddle pan piping hot.

On a platter, place the watermelon slices, top with the avocado, green olives, feta, mint, honey and lemon juice. Drizzle with the infused oil and season. For an extra touch of green, add some rocket, if liked.

1 tbsp olive oil

1 mini watermelon, cut into thick slices

2 avocados, peeled, stoned/ pitted and sliced

100 g/3½ oz. green olives, stoned/pitted

100 g/3½ oz. feta cheese

10 g/⅓ oz. fresh mint leaves

1 tbsp runny honey

juice of ½ lemon (or to taste)

2–3 tbsp pink pepper and Aleppo chilli-infused olive oil (see below)

100 g/3½ oz. rocket/arugula (optional)

sea salt and freshly ground black pepper

INFUSED OIL

100 ml/3½ oz. extra virgin olive oil

½ tbsp pink peppercorns, crushed

1 tbsp Aleppo chilli/hot red pepper flakes

SERVES 4

STEAK SALAD WITH PECORINO DRESSING

This steak salad pairs perfectly with extra thin and crispy fries and a nice glass of red wine.

Place all the ingredients for the dressing in a blender and blend to combine. Season to taste and set aside.

For the steak, mix the Worcestershire sauce and Dijon mustard together and brush onto the steak, season well and drizzle with 2 tablespoons of the oil.

Preheat a lightly greased barbecue or chargrill pan over a high heat. Barbecue the steak, turning once, until browned and cooked to your liking (5 minutes each side for medium-rare). Set aside to rest for 10 minutes and slice when ready to serve.

While the steak is resting, season the courgettes and brush with the olive oil. Griddle for a few minutes on each side.

Arrange the lettuce on a platter and drizzle over the dressing. Top with the sliced steak, griddled courgettes and scatter over the dill. Serve with super skinny fries, if liked.

2 tbsp Worcestershire sauce

1 tbsp Dijon mustard

800 g/1¾ lb. flank or skirt steak, trimmed, room temperature

2 courgettes/zucchini, thinly sliced lengthways

4 tbsp olive oil, plus extra to drizzle

3 baby cos lettuce, trimmed, leaves separated

sea salt and freshly ground black pepper

PECORINO DRESSING

2 anchovy fillets in oil, drained and finely chopped

80 g/3 oz. pecorino, plus extra to serve

juice of ½ lemon

160 ml/⅔ cup olive oil

TO SERVE

freshly chopped dill

super skinny fries, sprinkled with thyme (optional)

SERVES 4

AUBERGINE WITH CUCUMBER & BUTTERMILK DRESSING

This salad has depth and freshness at the same time. The aubergines/ eggplant are roasted to bring out their deep earthiness and the cucumbers paired with the buttermilk dressing make a refreshing, yet satisfying salad.

Heat 1 tablespoon of the olive oil in a pan over a medium–high heat and fry the shallots on both sides for about 5 minutes until tender and slightly charred and crisp around the edges. Season with salt.

Add 2 tablespoons of the olive oil and half of the aubergine slices and arrange in a single layer. Season lightly with salt. Cook, without moving, for about 3 minutes until browned underneath. Turn, cook on the second side for about 2 minutes until browned and tender. Transfer to a large bowl. Add the remaining 2 tablespoons of the oil to the pan and repeat with the remaining aubergine slices. Leave to cool slightly.

To make the dressing, whisk the buttermilk, lemon juice and zest, mustard, honey and several grinds of pepper in a medium bowl until smooth and stir through the shallot.

Place the aubergine in a bowl, then add the cucumbers, parsley and chives. Toss well and season with salt and black pepper. Gently fold in the avocado.

Transfer to a platter and drizzle with several spoonfuls of the dressing (you don't need to use all of it) and finish with the rocket.

5 tbsp olive oil

4 shallots, peeled and halved

8 baby aubergines/eggplant, halved

4 baby cucumbers, shaved lengthways or chopped

20 g/⅔ cup fresh parsley, leaves picked

10 g/⅓ cup fresh chives, finely chopped

1 avocado, peeled, stoned/ pitted and cut into chunks

100 g/2 cups rocket/arugula, stems removed

sea salt and freshly ground black pepper

BUTTERMILK DRESSING

100 ml/scant ½ cup buttermilk

juice and zest of 1 lemon

1 tsp Dijon mustard

1 tsp honey

1 shallot, finely chopped

SERVES 4

OREGANO HALLOUMI, WITH SHAVED ASPARAGUS IN AGRODOLCE DRESSING

This salty, sweet and sour salad with the griddled halloumi, fresh shaved asparagus and sweet and sour agrodolce dressing is sure to impress anyone at your table.

Place the halloumi in a bowl with the olive oil, sumac and oregano and leave to marinate while cooking the peppers.

Preheat the oven to 220°C/200°C fan/425°F/Gas 7. Line a large, flat baking sheet with baking paper.

Halve the peppers and arrange on the baking sheet, cut-side down. Roast for 30–35 minutes until the skin is shrivelled and lightly blistered. Set aside to cool completely before peeling. Once cooled, slice into strips.

For the dressing, heat the vinegar and sugar in a small saucepan to a simmer over a medium heat, stirring to dissolve the sugar. Place the onion in a bowl, pour the vinegar mixture over, add the sultanas and set aside to steep.

Meanwhile, roast the pine nuts on an oven tray, shaking the pan occasionally, until golden. Transfer to the onion mixture, along with the lemon segments and dill and set aside until ready to serve.

Place the shaved asparagus and courgette on a serving platter with the fregola and season well. Top with the tomatoes and red pepper strips and leave to sit while cooking the halloumi.

For the halloumi, heat a frying pan/skillet to a medium-high heat and add some of the oil from the halloumi marinade. Fry the halloumi in batches, for about 2 minutes on each side, then add to the other salad ingredients. Dress with the agrodolce dressing and serve.

2 x blocks halloumi, sliced

3 tbsp olive oil

1 tsp sumac

3 sprigs of fresh oregano, leaves picked

2 red (bell) peppers

1 bunch of asparagus, woody ends trimmed and shaved

1 courgette/zucchini, thinly sliced

100 g/3½ oz. fregola, cooked and cooled

200 g/7 oz. mixed heirloom tomatoes, coarsely chopped

AGRODOLCE DRESSING

180 ml/¾ cup white wine vinegar

50 g/¼ cup brown sugar

1 red onion, finely chopped

50 g/⅓ cup sultanas/golden raisins

60 g/½ cup pine nuts

2 lemons, segmented

20 g/⅔ cup fresh dill, chopped

SERVES 4

BUCKWHEAT TABBOULEH WITH BEANS & GRAINY LAMB MEATBALLS

Using buckwheat in this mixed bean tabbouleh makes it a great gluten-free alternative. This can be a great sharing salad with the grainy lamb meatballs, or part of a larger sharing table with the addition of other elements. Roasting the garlic in the dressing makes it more mellow and just delicious.

Start by making the roast garlic dressing. Preheat the oven to 220°C/200°C fan/425°F/Gas 7.

Wrap the garlic tightly in foil, place on a baking sheet and roast for 30–35 minutes until tender and caramelized. When cool enough to handle, squeeze the garlic from the skins into a bowl (discard the skins), whisk in the oil, lemon juice and zest, and sumac, season to taste and set aside.

To make the meatballs, add the bulgur, lamb, garlic, spices and a pinch each of salt and pepper to a food processor and pulse to combine well. With slightly wet hands, shape the lamb mixture into golf ball-sized balls, then massage them a little to create elasticity, and shape into ovals. Place on a tray and refrigerate until required.

Fry the meatballs in a frying pan/skillet for about 8–10 minutes (in 2 batches), turning occasionally, until golden and cooked through. Keep warm.

To make the tabbouleh, combine the buckwheat, beans, peas, green beans, pumpkin seeds and herbs in a bowl, drizzle with dressing, season to taste and toss to combine. Scatter the red onion, pickled chillies and pine nuts over the top.

Serve the tabbouleh with the meatballs and pita breads sprinkled with sumac on the side.

BUCKWHEAT TABBOULEH

150 g/scant 1 cup buckwheat, cooked and cooled

400-g/14-oz. can butter beans/lima beans

200 g/1½ cups broad/fava beans, skins removed

200 g/1½ cups frozen peas, blanched and refreshed

100 g/3½ oz. mixed fine green beans, blanched and refreshed

30 g/¼ cup toasted pumpkin seeds

1 bunch fresh flat-leaf parsley, finely chopped

1 bunch fresh mint, leaves picked and finely chopped

½ red onion, thinly sliced

30 g/2 tbsp pickled red chillies/chiles, chopped (optional)

2 tbsp toasted pine nuts

ROAST GARLIC DRESSING

1 bulb garlic

60 ml/¼ cup extra-virgin olive oil

finely grated zest and freshly squeezed juice of 2 lemons

1 tsp sumac

GRAINY LAMB MEATBALLS

75 g/scant ½ cup bulgur, soaked overnight in water in the fridge

500 g/1 lb. 2 oz. minced/ground lamb

2 garlic cloves, crushed

2 tsp paprika

½ tsp ground cloves

½ tsp ground cinnamon

sea salt and freshly ground black pepper

vegetable oil, for shallow-frying

TO SERVE

warmed pita breads

sumac, to sprinkle

SERVES 4

BURNT PLUMS & FIGS WITH BURRATA, SESAME NUT CRUMBLE & A BASIL & PARSLEY DRESSING

A little more adventurous but a really nice way to serve a deep, sweet, nutty and fresh salad. This salad actually comes in two parts, which are delicious served together, but also work well on their own if preferred.

Add a little butter to the halved plums and cook flesh-side down in a frying pan/skillet for about 20 minutes until burned and starting to cook through. Turn over, drizzle with the honey and cook for 5 minutes, then set aside.

Repeat with the figs, but for less time, about 5 minutes.

Preheat the oven to 200°C/180°C fan/400°F/Gas 6 for the sesame nut crumble.

On a lined baking tray, place the pistachios, sesame seeds, pumpkin seeds and green olives. Drizzle with the honey and olive oil, season with sea salt and bake for 8–10 minutes, mixing through halfway. Once golden, leave to cool, then roughly chop into a crumb and set aside.

For the dressing, blitz all the ingredients in a blender until smooth. Season well and set aside.

Place the plums and figs and all their juices on a plate and top with one of the burrata. Sprinkle over the sesame crumb and drizzle with some of the dressing.

Place the tomatoes and remaining burrata on a separate serving plate, top with basil and drizzle over some more dressing. Serve immediately with the plums and figs.

100 g/½ cup butter

6 plums, halved and stoned/pitted

2 tbsp pine honey

6 figs, halved

SESAME NUT CRUMBLE

100 g/¾ cup shelled pistachios

50 g/⅓ cup sesame seeds

50 g/⅓ cup pumpkin seeds

50 g/½ cup stoned/pitted green olives

50 ml/3½ tbsp pine honey

50 ml/3½ tbsp olive oil

sea salt and freshly ground black pepper

BASIL & PARSLEY DRESSING

20 g/⅔ cup basil, stems removed

20 g/⅔ cup flat-leaf parsley, stems removed

2 garlic cloves, crushed

grated zest and juice of 1 lemon

1 tsp honey

100 ml/scant ½ cup olive oil

TO SERVE

2 x burrata

sliced tomatoes

fresh basil leaves

SERVES 2

INSALATA TRICOLORE

Always classic and always the favourite. This is the most classic of combinations that is loved the world around and back.

Remove the tomatoes from the vine and wash. Drain and slice or cut into halves, depending on sizes.

Slice the avocado into long strips and layer on a large serving dish. Arrange the mozzarella slices around the avocado or place the burrata in the centre). Scatter the tomatoes over the plate.

To serve, drizzle with olive oil and season. Drizzle with balsamic vinegar, tear the basil leaves and sprinkle on top of the salad. Serve with rocket, if using, focaccia and parma ham.

300 g/11½ oz. mixed tomatoes

1 extra large ripe and ready avocado, peeled and stoned/pitted

8 slices of buffalo mozzarella (or 1 burrata)

2 tbsp extra virgin olive oil

1 tbsp balsamic vinegar

6–8 fresh basil leaves

30 g/¾ cup rocket/arugula, stems trimmed (optional)

sea salt and freshly ground black pepper

focaccia and parma ham, to finish

SERVES 2 TO SHARE

WARM WINTER SALAD WITH HERB & WALNUT DRESSING

Seek comfort in this deliciously warming salad, rich in herb and nutty notes from the dressing, which works wonderfully well with crisp radicchio and hearty butter/lima beans.

Preheat the oven to 220°C/200°C fan/425°F/Gas 7.

Toss the cauliflower with 3 tablespoons of the olive oil and some salt and pepper in a bowl. Transfer to a roasting tray and cook in the preheated oven for 15 minutes.

Stir in the red onions, garlic, rosemary and lemon slices. Drizzle over the remaining oil and roast for a further 10 minutes.

Add the radicchio wedges and cook for a further 5 minutes.

Place onto a serving dish, add the butter beans and top with a pinch of sumac to finish.

To make the dressing, combine the walnut oil, walnut pieces and garlic in a saucepan over a low heat for a few minutes until fragrant.

Stir in the sherry vinegar and maple syrup. Remove from the heat, then season with salt and pepper and whisk to bring everything together. Stir in the parsley and basil and use to dress the salad.

1 cauliflower, cut into florets

7 tbsp olive oil

2 red onions, cut into wedges

4 garlic cloves, smashed

3 sprigs of fresh rosemary

2 lemons, thinly sliced into rounds

2 radicchio, cut into wedges

1 400-g/14-oz. can butter/ lima beans, drained and rinsed

a pinch of ground sumac

sea salt and freshly ground black pepper

HERB & WALNUT DRESSING

6 tbsp walnut oil

35 g/¼ cup walnut halves, toasted

1 garlic clove, crushed

3 tbsp sherry vinegar

½ tsp maple syrup

1 tbsp freshly chopped parsley leaves

1 tbsp freshly chopped basil

SERVES 6

CHORIZO, ROASTED CHICKPEAS, PRESERVED LEMON & PARSLEY SALAD

An all-in-one roasted, crispy, earthy and delicious salad that can be served straight from the roasting tray or on a platter.

Preheat the oven to 220°C/200°C fan/425°F/Gas 7.

Place the mini chorizo sausages, chickpeas, cauliflower and cherry tomatoes on a baking sheet lined with baking paper. Drizzle with the olive oil and season with salt and pepper.

Roast in the oven for 25 minutes or until the chorizo is cooked through, the chickpeas are golden and the cherry tomatoes soft. Leave to cool, then place on a platter with all the juices.

Meanwhile, combine the dressing ingredients in a bowl and season with pepper to taste.

Add the wild salad leaves to the platter and drizzle with the dressing. Finish with black olives and serve with chunky bread on the side.

200 g/7 oz. mini chorizo sausages

1 x 400 g/14 oz. can chickpeas/ garbanzo beans, drained

200 g/7 oz. sprouting cauliflower or florets

200 g/1 cup cherry tomatoes on the vine

3 tbsp olive oil

100 g/2 cups wild salad leaves

50 g/½ cup stoned/pitted black olives, chopped

sea salt and freshly ground black pepper

PRESERVED LEMON DRESSING

½ preserved lemon rind, finely chopped

30 g/1 cup fresh parsley, finely chopped

1 long red chilli/chile, finely chopped

60 ml/¼ cup extra-virgin olive oil

juice of ½ lemon (or to taste)

SERVES 2

TOASTED MIXED GRAINS WITH LEMON LABNE

Absolute heaven on a plate! It's hard to know where to begin – the toasted grains for added bite or the lemony creamy home-made labne, finished with sweet and sour pomegranate molasses. Pre-toasting the grains adds another element to this perfect dish.

Start the lemon labne the night before. Combine the yogurt, lemon zest and juice, garlic, salt and freshly ground black pepper (to taste) in a bowl, then transfer to a sieve/strainer lined with muslin. Place over a bowl to catch the liquid and refrigerate overnight to drain.

Dry-roast the spelt and faro in a frying pan/skillet for 1–2 minutes until nutty and fragrant. Tip the grains into a saucepan, cover with boiling water and simmer for 15–20 minutes until tender, then drain and refresh under cold running water. Drain well and transfer to a large bowl. Meanwhile, cook the quinoa in a pan of boiling salted water for 4–5 minutes, add the bulgur, cook for another minute, drain well and refresh under cold running water. Drain well and add to the spelt mixture.

Make the pomegranate dressing directly in the serving bowl by whisking all the ingredients together, then season to taste. In the same dish add the green lentils, pistachios, dried apricots, red onion and all the cooked grains. Season to taste and toss to combine. Gently mix through all the micro herbs and greens.

Place a dollop of labne on side plates and sprinkle with za'atar. Add some of the grainy mix, top with pomegranate seeds, then drizzle with olive oil.

50 g/⅓ cup spelt grain
50 g/⅓ cup faro
60 g/⅓ cup quinoa grains
60 g/⅓ cup bulgur
400-g/14-oz. can green lentils, drained
80 g/⅔ cup pistachios, coarsely chopped
75 g/½ cup dried apricots, coarsely chopped
1 red onion, thinly sliced
150 g/5½ oz. mixed micro herbs and leaves

LEMON LABNE
500 g/2¼ cups Greek yogurt
grated zest and freshly squeezed juice of 1 lemon
1 garlic clove, crushed
1½ tsp salt
freshly ground black pepper

POMEGRANATE DRESSING
80 ml/⅓ cup extra-virgin olive oil
2 tbsp red wine vinegar
freshly squeezed juice of 1 lemon
2 tbsp pomegranate molassess
½ pomegranate, seeds only
a pinch of za'atar
sea salt and freshly ground black pepper

TO SERVE
1 tbsp za'atar
½ pomegranate, seeds only
olive oil, to drizzle

muslin/cheesecloth

SERVES 4–6

BEAN, SMOKED TROUT & NEW POTATO SALAD

This is lovely for a weekend lunch or buffet, alongside
a cheeseboard or some lovely fresh bread.

To make the dressing, mix all the ingredients together in a jar
or bowl and shake or mix well.

Cook the potatoes in boiling salted water for 10 minutes until just
tender, then drain, allow to cool slightly, then slice into rounds.

Cook the beans in a saucepan of boiling salted water for 10 minutes
until tender, then plunge into ice water and drain.

Toss the warm potatoes and beans together with half the spring onions
and parsley and half the dressing.

Spread out on a platter, then top with the smoked trout. Scatter over
the rest of the spring onions, drizzle with the remaining dressing and
serve, or leave everyone to help themselves.

500 g/1 lb. 2 oz. new potatoes

300 g/11½ oz. runner beans,
trimmed and sliced
diagonally

4 spring onions/scallions, sliced

½ bunch fresh parsley, roughly
chopped

200 g/7 oz. smoked trout

10 g/⅓ cup mini herbs, leaves
and edible flowers

DRESSING

50 ml/¼ cup extra-virgin
olive oil

juice of ½ lemon

2 tbsp crème fraiche

2 tsp wholegrain mustard

1 tbsp horseradish (optional)

SERVES 4

WARM FREGOLA SALAD, WITH ROASTED MUSHROOMS

These slow-roasted mushrooms are warming, comforting and super delicious.

Preheat the oven to 220°C/200°C fan/425°F/Gas 7. Place the mushrooms in a single layer in a roasting dish. Season with salt and pepper, then scatter over the remaining ingredients. Cover with foil and roast for 1 hour, uncovering for the last 20 minutes, until just tender.

At the same time, bake the Parmesan crisps. In a medium bowl, stir together the cheeses. Spoon heaped tablespoons of the mixture onto 2 baking sheets lined with baking paper, spacing them apart. Slightly flatten each mound and bake for about 8–10 minutes until golden brown. Leave to cool completely on the baking sheets before carefully removing with a spatula – they may break if you try to move them while still warm.

Cook the fregola in a large saucepan of boiling salted water for 6–8 minutes until almost al dente. Drain the fregola but do not rinse, reserving 250 ml/1 cup of the cooking liquid.

Heat the oil in a saucepan over a medium heat. Add the onion and sauté, stirring, for 5 minutes. Add the garlic and sauté for a 3–5 minutes until soft. Add the wine and simmer for 5 minutes until the pan is almost dry. Add the stock and bay leaves and bring to a simmer. Add the fregola and simmer for about 5 minutes, stirring, until the fregola is tender and the broth has thickened. Season and add some of the reserved cooking liquid, if needed, to moisten. Turn down the heat and stir through the sun-dried tomato paste.

Stir through the basil, top with rocket and drizzle with lemon juice and olive oil. Serve with the roasted mushrooms and Parmesan crisps.

700 g/1 lb. 9 oz. mixed Portobello and Portobellini mushrooms

5 golden shallots, thinly sliced

3 garlic cloves, thinly sliced

45 ml/3 tbsp extra virgin olive oil

50 g/3½ tbsp butter, coarsely chopped

30 g/¼ cup lightly toasted hazelnuts, coarsely chopped

8 fresh thyme sprigs, plus extra to serve

30 ml/2 tbsp hazelnut oil

sea salt and freshly ground black pepper

PARMESAN CRISPS

100 g/3½ oz. Parmesan, finely grated

100 g/3½ oz. Parmesan, coarsely shredded

WARM FREGOLA SALAD

300 g/10½ oz. fregola

2 tbsp olive oil

1 onion, finely chopped

3 garlic cloves, crushed

200 ml/generous ¾ cup white wine

350 ml/1½ cups vegetable stock

2 bay leaves

2 tbsp sun-dried tomato paste

1 bunch fresh basil, leaves only

200 g/7 oz. wild rocket/arugula

freshly squeezed juice of 1 lemon

drizzle of extra virgin olive oil

SERVES 4

KALE, CELERIAC & BEETROOT SALAD WITH BASIL CAESAR DRESSING

Just a touch healthier and definitely a twist on a traditional Caesar salad, this is a perfect base for some shredded chicken or sliced boiled eggs. As part of this feast I have kept it simple, but as a main meal, the addition of protein would make it more substantial.

To make the dressing, whizz together the eggs, garlic, lemon juice, Dijon mustard, Worcestershire sauce, anchovies and the basil in a small food processor. Season well with sea salt and black pepper, then keep the food processor running and gradually pour in the olive oil until the dressing becomes really thick and glossy. Set aside.

Preheat the oven to 220°C/200°C fan/425°F/Gas 7.

To make the croûtons, chop the slices of rye bread into rough cubes. Toss the croutons with the olive oil in a bowl and season with salt and pepper. Spread the cubes out in one layer on a baking sheet lined with baking paper and bake in the preheated oven for 10–15 minutes until toasted. Set aside to cool.

Assembly can be done last minute, but prepare the celeriac in advance by storing it in some water with a squeeze of lemon juice in it to stop the celeriac from discolouring.

To serve, lay the kale, lettuce leaves, beetroot, celeriac, croûtons and Parmesan shavings on a platter, then drizzle over the dressing. Top with shredded chicken or sliced eggs, if using.

½ celeriac, peeled and grated

a handful of kale

3 Cos lettuce leaves, cut into large pieces

2 beetroot/beets, peeled and grated

20 g/¾ oz. shaved Parmesan

BASIL CAESAR DRESSING

2 eggs

1 garlic clove, crushed

juice of 1 lemon

2 tsp Dijon mustard

a dash of Worcestershire sauce

2 anchovies in olive oil

a handful of fresh basil

200 ml/scant 1 cup olive oil

sea salt and freshly ground black pepper

RYE BREAD CROÛTONS

2 slices of rye sourdough bread

1 tbsp olive oil

TO SERVE (OPTIONAL)

shredded poached chicken

7-minute boiled/cooked eggs

SERVES 6

WARM CAULIFLOWER & POTATO SALAD

So many gorgeous ingredients together on one platter! This is delicious eaten cold, but is best just warm with the feta, lemon and dill.

Preheat the oven to 220°C/200°C fan/425°F/Gas 7.

In a large, deep baking pan, toss the potatoes with half of the olive oil until well coated. Roast in the preheated oven for 20 minutes, then add the cauliflower and garlic. Season the vegetables well with salt and pepper and stir to make sure they are well coated in oil. Continue roasting for another 20–25 minutes, until the potatoes are cooked through and the cauliflower is starting to colour.

In a bowl, mix the remaining olive oil with the lemon zest and juice, add the dill and set aside.

Put a frying pan/skillet over a medium-high heat, then add the cavolo nero with a few tablespoons of water and cook until just softened. Transfer to a colander to drain any excess water.

Arrange the cavolo nero on a platter and top with the roasted potatoes and cauliflower. Finish with the spring onions and feta cheese, drizzle with the lemon-dill dressing and sprinkle with dried chilli flakes, if using. Serve warm.

500 g/1 lb. 2 oz. purple potatoes or normal potatoes, scrubbed, skin left on and roughly chopped

60 ml/¼ cup olive oil

350 g/12 oz. cauliflower, cut into small florets

2 garlic cloves, finely chopped

grated zest and freshly squeezed juice of 1 lemon

small bunch fresh dill, finely chopped

100 g/3½ oz. cavolo nero, stems removed and roughly chopped

3 spring onions/scallions, thinly sliced

100 g/3½ oz. feta, crumbled

1 tsp dried chilli/hot red pepper flakes (optional)

sea salt and freshly ground black pepper

SERVES 4

INDEX

ACKNOWLEDGEMENTS

Thank you to the super talented RPS team who are the most wonderful people in the business. Leslie Harrington, Megan Smith, Julia Charles and Abi Waters.

Thank you to Mowie Kay – as always the most fabulous photographer that makes food look like a piece of art. Lauren Miller – who just knows how to choose the right props to bring the scene together. Sadie Albuquerque – for your calm and gentle assistance and generally being so lovely to be around.

Dedicated to Matthew Whitaker my chief taste tester.